D1512679

POULTRY SIGNALS

A PRACTICAL GUIDE FOR BIRD FOCUSED POULTRY FARMING

Monique Bestman • Marko Ruis • Jos Heijmans • Koos van Middelkoop

C r e d i t s   <u>**Poultry Signals**</u>

Editor
Jan Hulsen, Vetvice Groep

Authors
Monique Bestman
Marko Ruis
Jos Heijmans
Koos van Middelkoop

Final editing
Ton van Schie

English Translation
Agrolingua

Photography
Photography Cover: Marcel Bekken
Photography
(unless credited otherwise)
Louis Bolk Instituut, Livestock Research
Wageningen UR, GD
Other photographs:
Alpharma (107bl, 107br), Aviagen (88bl, 88br), Marcel
Bekken (cover), C. Bennet (44r), Marcel Berendsen (achter-
zijde b, 4, 8b, 9tr, 11t, 24t, 24b, 25, 26r, 27tl, 34br, 34l,
45br, 45t, 48l, 48tr, 49 (6,7), 54b, 55tl, 56, 57br, 58bl,
58bm, 58br, 59, 60l, 70tl, 73br, 90, 97bl, 97br), C. Berg
(81r), Bloemendaal Eierhandel (65mr), Ron Jöerissen
(57bl), Henk Heidekamp (54t), Interbroed leghennen (50,
51, 61mr), Berry Lott (85ml, 85mr), Jac Matijssen (14l),
Bastiaan Meerburg (93m), Frank van Merle, Aviagen (89),
Koos van Middelkoop (78tl), Pas Reform (44l), Henk
Rodenboog (86br, 86bl, 87tr), Schippers BVBA (101br),
Arthur Slaats (77bl, 77br, 82), Hilly Speelman (36t), Rob
van Veldhuizen (93b), Vencomatic (7lm, 33, 69b, 76b),
Verbeek (94b), Ron Verdel (39ml), Zonne-Ei-Farm B.V (7t)
b= bottom, t = top, m = middle, l = left, r = right

Illustrations
Marinette Hoogendoorn

Design
Dick Rietveld, Erik de Bruin, Varwig Design

Special thanks to:
Peter van Agt, Marleen Boerjan, Pieter Bouw, Mijndert
van den Brink, Hilko Ellen, Rick van Emous, Marrit
van Engen, Teun Fabri, Thea Fiks, Niels Geraerts, Arjan
Gussinklo, Jan van Harn, Wim Hoeve, Jan Hulsen, Ingrid
de Jong, René Kieftenbelt, Gerjan Klok, Cécile Korevaar,
Marinus van Krimpen, Pieter Kruit, Jan en Marcel Kuijpers,
Ferry Leenstra, Sander Lourens, Jac Matijsen, Monique
Mul, Bert van Nijhuis, Kees van Ooijen, Wim Peters, Dr.
David Pollock, Bianca Reindsen, Berry Reuvekamp, Henk
Rodenboog, Jorine Rommers, Piet Simons, Arthur Slaats,
Alex Spieker, André van Straaten, Otto van Tuil, Cor van de
Ven, Jan-Paul Wagenaar, Ruud van Wee, Sible Westendorp.

Roodbont Publishers B.V.
P.O. Box 4103
NL-7200 BC Zutphen
Telephone: +31 (0)575 54 56 88
Fax: +31 (0)575 54 69 90
E-mail: info@roodbont.nl
www.roodbont.com

LOUIS BOLK
I N S T I T U U T

Hoofdstraat 24
3972 LA Driebergen
Telephone: +31 (0)343 52 38 60
Fax: +31 (0)343 51 56 11
E-mail: info@louisbolk.nl
www.louisbolk.nl

LIVESTOCK RESEARCH
WAGENINGEN UR

P.O. Box 65
8200 AB Lelystad
Telephone: +31 (0)320 23 82 38
Fax: +31 (0)320 23 80 50
E-mail: info.livestockresearch@wur.nl
www.livestockresearch.wur.nl

.GD

P.O. Box 9
7400 AA Deventer
Telephone: +31 (0)900 1770
Fax: +31 (0)570 63 41 04
E-mail: info@gddeventer.com
www.gddeventer.com

The authors and publisher have compiled this publication with the
greatest care and to the best of our knowledge. However, the authors
and publisher do not accept any liability due to damage of any kind
resulting from actions and/or decisions based on this information.

ISBN 978-90-8740-079-8

Contents

Focus on chickens

Poultry keeping is all about the chickens. So providing a comfortable home for them and looking after them properly is a basic requirement. It's also important to work economically and neatly. Poultry Signals is about how to house and care for chickens in the best possible way, so the focus is always on the chicken. What is a chicken and what are its needs in terms of health, welfare and production? Poultry keepers who are aware of these needs check on their birds properly several times a day, making sure they cover the whole flock. They respond promptly to every irregularity and warning sign, and they have many well defined routines to help them. They also make sure their work is not too time-consuming, their working conditions are pleasant and their inventory is kept in good condition.

Everyone can learn how to observe and understand chickens better so that they can manage their birds' health, welfare and production better. Some people have a natural ability to observe and understand chickens. Others have to go to a lot of trouble to learn. But everyone improves with practice.

Many people find that when it comes to observing and assessing their birds they can't see the wood for the trees . The goal is to see the wood *and* the trees. They are so involved in the farm that they no longer notice irregularities because they are so used to seeing them. So identify your own blind spots and eliminate them. Open your mind to new things. Be critical. And don't be afraid to change.

An important question a good entrepreneur regularly asks himself is: am I getting the very best out of everything? Or could I be getting even more?

Changing situations

The laying hen sector is in a state of flux. Cage systems are being phased out. So many laying hen farmers will have to make a choice (if they have not already done so): do I go for an enriched cage system or an aviary system? Do I go free-range or even organic? The choice of system is up to the poultry farmer, and will depend on personal preference, financial returns and the environmental options he has. A new system places different demands on the poultry farmer. The more opportunity chickens get to express their natural behaviour, the more you can read them. But not only that: the more you will have to manage the bird itself instead of the system it is kept in.

Poultry Signals hones your ability to pick up signals from chickens and use them to manage and improve them.

Train yourself to look and see

Proper care of your birds begins with critical observation. Look with awareness. Take a step back (sometimes literally). You can't look at things with awareness if you are doing something else at the same time. Stop and think about the signals your birds are sending. The longer you spend on this, the more subtle signals you will pick up on. It takes skill to see signals before the consequences reveal themselves.

The red thread running through this book is 'look, think and act'. The three basic questions a poultry farmer must keep on asking themselves are:

1. **What am I observing?**
2. **Why is this happening?**
3. **What should I do?**

Production – health - behaviour

Production, health and behaviour are as firmly interlinked as the sides of a triangle.

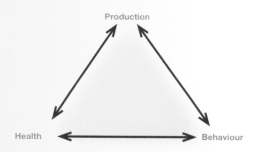

The one affects the other. Production is the central objective of any farmer or entrepreneur. Production is closely related to behaviour and health. A distressed flock wastes energy. Stressed birds are susceptible to disease, and a sick bird lays less. You can tell that a bird is sick by the way it behaves. Production, in turn, impacts on health and behaviour, weaker birds have lower resistance, and heavier birds can dominate the group. Finally, chickens have certain behavioural needs. If they are unable to meet these needs, stress and lower resistance may ensue. So you can always follow the triangle from different starting points.

Not a manual

Poultry Signals is not a manual listing standards for all aspects of poultry farming. It is a guide that will help you look after your birds properly and translate their signals into actions that will help you run your business better. The book is written in a form that we hope will invite you to dip into it regularly, giving you lots of new ideas each time.

A look at the different sectors

Although it is difficult to bring the different sectors together in one book, we have managed to do just that in *Poultry Signals*, since many of the aspects apply equally to all of them. In the first, long chapter we take a close look at chickens in general: their genetics, anatomy and behaviour. In the chapter on Health we discuss health and disease problems that can arise for all types of poultry.

Besides, you can always learn something from the other sectors if you are open to doing so.

Top athletes

The production of eggs and meat is a top athletic achievement for the birds. It goes without saying that there is a big difference between layers and broilers. The poultry in different subsectors and even different systems can be compared with different kinds of athletes. Athletes also come in all shapes and sizes depending on their discipline.

Laying hen: the stayer
Like long-distance runners, this type of bird needs to perform for a long time and therefore needs stamina.

Broiler: the sprinter
Like a sprinter, this hen has to perform for a short period of time.

Layers in alternative systems: the steeple-chaser
Non-caged layers are faced with different challenges from caged birds. So their lives can be compared with a steeple-chase.

Differences within sectors

Layers: less and less difference

Twenty years ago layers could be classed as light-weight and medium-weight. Light-weight hens were usually white and laid white eggs, and medium-weight birds were brown and laid brown eggs. White hens often laid slightly more eggs, needed less food and were more jumpy, active or nervous.

There is still a difference between white and brown, but the birds have since become more alike in weight, and both types are now kept in caged and non-caged systems. Medium-weight Silvers have also made an appearance in recent years. These birds have white feathers interspersed with the occasional brown one. They lay brown eggs and have the weight and nature of brown hens.

Broilers: traditional versus slow-growing

The most logical way of categorising broilers is traditional versus slow-growing. Traditional broilers are the most widely used. They weigh 2.5 kg at 6 weeks. White-feathered birds are selected because the breast meat will be the nice white colour favoured by consumers. The birds spend most of their time eating and grow fast. During their lives they become less and less active. The parent birds are put on a restricted diet at the rearing stage because overweight birds don't live so long and produce fewer hatching eggs.

Slow-growing broilers only weigh 2.5 kg after 9 weeks. Because they don't need to be top athletes they are less susceptible to disease, they have fewer respiratory and digestive problems and mortality rates are lower. Slow-growing broilers are kept in 'alternative systems' with more room and often with a 'winter garden' or range. They are more active than traditional broilers. They are largely white, but you do sometimes get the occasional speckled or brown one. The fathers are the same as those of traditional broilers, but the mothers are dwarf mother birds whose feed intake is kept limited.

In the past white chickens were mainly kept in cages. These will soon be banned. So-called colony-housing is a permitted alternative.

Brown hens are often slightly heavier than white ones so they need slightly more maintenance feed.

These birds are also often referred to as 'white on the outside, brown on the inside' because of their white appearance and other characteristics of brown breeds.

Slow-growing broilers

CHAPTER 1

Seeing more by looking more closely

If you only look at technical aspects such as laying percentages and egg quality, growth or feed and water consumption, you run the risk of missing important signals and being overtaken by events. You can pick up these signals from the chickens themselves and from their appearance, behaviour, manure and eggs.

In a nice healthy flock you will want to identify irregularities as soon as possible so as to avoid problems.

Use all your senses. Even before you enter the poultry house, you'll hear whether the hens sound different. Stand outside the door for a moment; don't go inside straight away. When you go in, you'll smell whether there is a problem with the manure or the ventilation. Use your eyes and ears to see and hear how active the birds are and whether they are reacting more, less or differently to your arrival than usual. Also use your senses to observe the heat and cold in the poultry house. Every irregularity needs to be attended to.

Farm blindness

You can only recognise irregularities if you know what is normal. You will learn what is normal by observing as often and as objectively as possible.

But be aware of the dangers of farm blindness. Farm blindness is when you see the situation on your own farm as the norm. Limit farm blindness by talking to colleagues and advisers. Act on critical comments.

Limit farm blindness by talking to colleagues and advisers.

Picking up the signals

You can pick up a lot from a flock while you are cleaning, collecting floor eggs and scattering grain. But make sure you also do some inspections without doing something else at the same time. You will be more aware of the signals because you are giving the hens and their environment your full attention. So don't combine an inspection with another activity like cleaning, collecting floor eggs or scattering grain. Activities - but also moods - detract from this. You will also disrupt the hens' behaviour, causing relevant signals to be lost. The chickens will also react less to your presence if you come into the house more often without doing anything specific.

An inspection is a tour of the whole house. Make sure you pay attention to all the birds. So look everywhere: front, back, middle, bottom, top.

Look from flock to chicken

Start your inspection by observing the whole flock. How are they spread out in the space? How are they using the different parts of the house? Are they avoiding certain places, maybe because the climate is bad there (draught, cold)? Try to spot the differences between birds. Are they uniform? How do they differ? In alertness, condition or in another way? Pick up birds that seem different and take a closer look. If you discover an irregularity, see whether it is an incidental case or a signal of a bigger, underlying problem. Also pick up some birds at random and assess them. Irregularities are not always immediately evident.

Things you observe in detail can only be properly assessed in their context. So look from chicken to flock as well. Sometimes you will need to take a step back to be able to see things better.

Put a chair in the house and sit on it for a few minutes at regular intervals to observe the birds. Only then will you pick up on any irregular behaviour.

Watch the chain feeder and make sure all the birds go to feed and that there are none that keep running back and forth. All the hens must be able to feed.

This hen is not healthy and is a source of trouble. Take this animal out of the flock.

Using the signals

Use what you see to improve your flock management. Ask the following questions about everything you see:

1. **What am I seeing (hearing, smelling, feeling)? What is the signal?**
2. **Why is this happening? What is the explanation?**
3. **What should I do? Can I leave it or should I take action?**

A genuine signal will be repeated. Think about what you are seeing and how it relates to the circumstances: does it happen often? At different times? To different birds? On other farms? Go and see for yourself or ask people. Also go and look in the evening and at night.

Know when risks are likely to occur and keep one step ahead by eliminating them or being extra alert if you are expecting them.

Risk birds

There will always be some risk birds in a flock, such as poorly developed ones. They will be the first to suffer from disease, lack of water or other shortages. These are the signal birds. The risk birds are the first ones to tell you that something is wrong. All the more reason to be alert to them. Risk birds also include those whose behaviour or appearance could cause problems. Not as a victim but as the cause. Think about which birds and problems they are in terms of your particular farm and how you can respond to them promptly.

Frightened or sick chickens in the nests will soil the eggs.

Frightened or sick chickens in the nests will soil the eggs.

1. Look at them both with and without doing other things.
2. Look at the whole flock, the individual chicken and then back to the flock.
3. Look for averages and extremes.
4. Look at the front, back and middle of the house. The same applies to processes such as feeding. Look at the front, middle and back of the feeder that is being filled. What is happening there?
5. Look at different times and in different circumstances.
6. At set times, stand still in the house; don't keep walking round the whole time.
7. Identify risk times, risk birds and risk places.

Risk analysis and action

Risk group	Risk	Action
Poorly developed birds	Low production	Pick out, separate or remove small birds
Floor layers	Vent pecking Even more floor eggs	Make corners and dark places unattractive with lighting (use electric wires). Collect floor eggs more often (the more often the better).
Frightened chickens that sit on top of or in the nests and are easily harassed	Less production Nest soiling	Determine and eliminate the stress factor. Pick out and separate.

Risk places

In every poultry house there are risk places where you can expect problems. Places you know could pose a risk should be a permanent part of your daily inspections. Make improvements to places that pose unnecessary risks. Examples of risk places include dark spots and corners, e.g. at partitions between sections, around laying nests, draughty places etc.

Risk times

There are certain times of the day or season or certain times during an inspection that can be risky. Known, recurring risk times are the feeding routines. Make sure your feeding machine and its weighing scale are working properly.

Risk times can also last for several days or weeks. The time when young hens come into lay is a risk time, for example. This is not only a risk time for the birds themselves but also for the operation of your system. If you open the nests too early, they can become contaminated. If you open them too late, the hens will lay outside the nests. Winter is a risk time as it is more difficult to keep the house

climate and the litter in optimal condition at that time of year. In summer both broilers and layers can suffer heat stress.

Unclassified notable observations

Sometimes you encounter things you don't immediately understand. Of course not every unclear signal will necessarily cause harm. A term for this unclassified notable observations (UNO, 'you know'). When you see such observations, you need to find out why they occur. You will learn most by trying to understand how good situations come about: in other words, what the success factors are.

Related signals

An indicator of the distribution of birds on perches at night is the height of the manure you find under the slats or on the various manure belts. If the distribution is uneven, then the chickens are roosting unevenly.

It is dark in the system: a risk place for floor eggs. Solution: install extra lighting.

→ flock looks fine
→ good condition
→ plumage stays well

No further remarks

Ask your advisers to record their observations in your logbook.

Signals in the records

You record a lot of data, but do you do enough with it? Checking at flock level should at the very least include accurate daily monitoring of water and feed consumption. Make it easier to spot changes by always recording the data at the same time of day. Generally a marked change in water consumption is the first signal that there is a health or feed problem (e.g. too salty). Or there may simply be something wrong with the water supply itself. A marked increase or reduction in feed intake is also cause for concern. This can indicate non-uniform feed.

Know yourself

You're on the go all day long: collecting eggs, doing inspections, doing paperwork, directing people, negotiating with customers and suppliers, and so on. Each of these tasks requires different personality traits. One poultry farmer will be more of an animal caretaker, the next will be more entrepreneurial, and yet another will be a more hands-on type. If you know yourself well, you can use your strong points and make sure your weaknesses are covered in other ways. Talking to advisers can help you decide which tasks you do best and what that means for the strategic choices you make in running your farm. Rather get someone else to do the tasks you are less good at or really don't like doing.

The animal caretaker, gets most satisfaction from working among the animals, but does he notice that there is other work to be done?

The hands-on person is fully focused on getting the work done. He tries to make conditions as pleasant as possible. But does he also pick up on problems with the birds in time?

The entrepreneur/manager concentrates on organising and running the farm. He needs to keep production up and keep revenues in line with costs. He also has to direct his personnel and maintain relationships with advisers, suppliers and customers. But does he spend enough time in the poultry shed?

Switching to an alternative

Switching from a cage to a free-range or aviary system means a whole new way of handling your chickens. In alternative systems, daily care takes twice as much attention and time. Animal care becomes an even more important aspect. The trick is to create conditions in which the chicken is as productive as possible. So you need to decide where and when to feed and water, what kind of lighting to install and where, etc. But also when you do things like collecting floor eggs. You need to have this all properly organised. In a cage system, the chicken farmer sets the timetable. In an alternative system, the chicken does.

And keep an eye open: every time you change something, watch how the hens react to it. They will tell you whether it is a good change. And perhaps you should think about keeping a different type of chicken?

What she wants

Every chicken has a number of basic needs that can be summarised as feed, water, light, air, rest, space and health. In every housing system and in every situation you need to check these conditions to make sure the chicken's needs are being met. The freer the system, the more attention you will have to pay to the various factors. Because even though a non-caged system may provide each chicken with enough space on average, if all the chickens are sitting on top of each other some will suffer. So does every bird have enough space all the time?

Wish list

To create an optimal environment for your chickens, you first need to know their needs. Scientists have established preferences in various ways. They look at how much effort they are prepared to make for things, for example by getting them to push a heavy door aside to get something, creep through a narrow opening or getting them to peck at a knob frequently. This gives a good picture of their needs.

Wish list
1. *Laying nest*
2. *Scratching*
3. *Perch*
4. *Dust bath*
5. *Extra space*

A chicken goes to just as much trouble with its laying nest just before it lays an egg as it does with feeding after fasting for eight hours. This tells us that a laying nest is an important need for a chicken at that time. So you can draw up a wish list. As a poultry farmer you should give the highest priority to whatever is at the top of the wish list.

These young hens are searching the wall for food. They are hungry and it is almost feeding time.

The five freedoms of the chicken:

1. Freedom from hunger, thirst and malnutrition
2. Freedom from physical discomfort
3. Freedom from pain, injury and disease
4. Freedom to express normal behaviour
5. Freedom from fear and distress

The EU regulation on animal welfare is based on these five freedoms.

J. Webster (1999)

How much space does a hen need?

Eating	450 cm²
Drinking	450 cm²
Scratching/foraging	800 cm²
Preening	1,100 cm²
Dust bathing	1,100 cm²
Laying	1,100 cm²
Resting	550 cm²

Source: Houden van hennen

On the left you can see how much space one laying hen needs to express her normal behaviour. If you take into account the time a hen spends doing something, the extent to which the hens want to express their normal behaviour simultaneously, the ideal distance between the hens in each type of behaviour and, finally, the layout of the house itself, then you'll conclude that the minimum area per bird should be 2.200 cm². Existing husbandry systems are therefore always a compromise between what chicken needs and what the farmer can offer.

Bird behaviour

It is important to understand your birds' natural behaviour, especially if they are not caged. Birds in a cage system don't display much behaviour, and some of the behaviours they do display have no particular consequences. With non-caged hens, certain behaviours could result in undesirable situations or even lead to major problems. Try to recognise undesirable behaviour in time and know what you can do to control it. Even more important is to set up your house and flock management to avoid undesirable behaviour like hens crawling over each other or laying eggs on the floor.

Roosters

Roosters can have a positive impact on the hens' behaviour. A rooster calms down quarrels between the hens. Hens look for food accompanied by roosters. Roosters also frequently accompany the hens to and from their sleeping places and entice them to suitable laying nests. Roosters are only useful if the hens and the roosters accept each other; in other words, if they are reared together. If they don't get on, the roosters may well end up hen-pecked in the laying nests. Make sure you introduce enough roosters. In the broiler industry (parent stock), hens and roosters are often reared separately, so pay extra attention when they are put together.

This rooster looks impressive and the hens leave him alone. The hens and roosters in this flock are not afraid of each other.

This rooster has been hen-pecked. This happened because the hens have no respect for him.

Group behaviour

A chicken is a social animal. She recognises about 80 others of her kind and knows who are the dominant birds in a small group. In larger groups, chickens are unable to recognise a clear pecking order among all the individuals. In large groups they tend to form sub-groups in which the birds know each other and have a set pecking order. These sub-groups will most likely keep to specific parts of the poultry houses. Birds that do not belong to a group and have no clear pecking order will wander among them. Heavier hens or hens with larger combs have a higher rank. Pecked and weaker hens retreat under the slats, into the laying nests or onto the racks. When doing your inspections, pay extra attention to these places to get a picture of the problem. Prevent this behaviour by creating additional refuges and resting places, for example on the top tier (with water only) or by installing perches on the slats.

Strict daily routine for layers

Non-caged chickens start each day by feeding and inspecting the nest box. Then they lay an egg. In the middle of the day they have a rest and take a dust bath. At the end of the day their scratching and feeding behaviour peaks. If there is any feather pecking, it will usually occur in the afternoon. The afternoon is therefore the most important time to offer distraction.

Do your inspections at other times as well, for example after feeding or in the evening when the birds are roosting. Chickens are creatures of habit and do different things throughout the day. If you do too many inspections at set times you could miss important signals because they are not demonstrating a particular behaviour at that time. For example, you will only observe distress caused by red mites after the chickens have gone to roost. Sometimes you will want the hens to be moving about so that you will notice any dead and passive ones. So always start your round when the feeding system starts running.

Laying an egg

Laying an egg is a whole production for a chicken every day.
1. The hen goes into the nest.
2. She sits there quietly for half an hour or more, often with her eyes closed.
3. She becomes increasingly restless, flicking up her tail repeatedly and spreading out the feathers on the laying stomach.
4. Suddenly she stands up and spreads her legs.
5. She strains at intervals and the egg starts to emerge.
6. The still damp egg pops out, followed by a red membrane.
7. After a few seconds the membrane is retracted and the vent closes.
8. The hen stands up over her egg and rests, beak open and panting.
9. She inspects the egg and leaves the nest, sometimes with a loud cackle.
10. The hen feeds and drinks and resumes her daily routine.

Phases 3 to 6 usually take no more than 30 seconds. Chickens are vulnerable during laying so you should leave them alone.

Daily routine

Night   **Morning**   **Afternoon**   **Evening**   **Night**

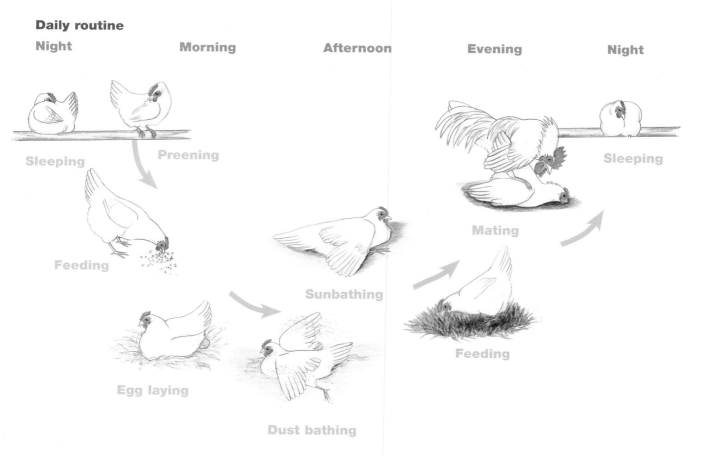

Sleeping

Preening

Feeding

Egg laying

Dust bathing

Sunbathing

Feeding

Mating

Sleeping

Behavioural needs: working and feeding

Chickens spend most of their time foraging for food. For them, feeding and scratching are inextricably linked. In the wild, they would spend half their time scratching and foraging. Even if they get their food from a feeder they still love scratching around. They also need to scratch around between feeds. Make sure they can do so by providing litter that is loose and dry. Then they will also be less inclined to pull out each other's feathers.

Scratching or scraping?

The term 'scratching' has several meanings. Scientists see it as foraging for food, while some poultry farmers describe it as 'running around in the litter'. Scientist call the latter activity 'dust bathing'.

How chickens spend their time in different environments

Type of chicken	Environment	% foraging for food and feeding	% abnormal behaviour	% resting behaviour
Jungle Fowl (wild chicken)	Wild	50	0	<50
Jungle Fowl	Zoo	60	0	10
Layer	Ground nest box	18	0	3
Layer	Cage	22	0	8
Chicks of layers that have run wild	Wild	53	0	39
Broiler parent birds	Unrestricted feed	8	0	50
Broiler parent birds	Restricted feed	<1	32	6
Broilers	Straw	10	0	70

Source: P. Koene, in Bels, 2006

Broilers and broiler parent birds

Broilers are inactive most of their time. Fast-growing varieties in particular can spend as much as 70% of their time on the ground. Broiler parent birds that receive an unrestricted diet are also inactive much of the time. But as soon as their feed is limited, everything revolves around feeding time and the quantity of feed. Because they spend less than ten minutes a day eating, feeding time makes up less than one per cent in the above table. You will see these birds spending a lot of time expressing abnormal behaviour such as overactivity, pecking at the empty feeder, running around a lot, drinking a lot and excessive aggression. It is essential to ensure that there is enough room for each bird to feed so as to avoid injury from pecking and scratching.

Behavioural needs: preening, dust bathing

Chickens keep their feathers in good condition by preening and dust bathing. Preening transfers the fat from the preen gland to the feathers. Dust bathing removes the old fat and any parasites with it. This improves the feather quality: the feathers remain looser and retain warmth better. Dust baths prevent the feathers from becoming brittle, reducing breakage. Chickens start dust bathing from 4-6 days. The dust bathing routine is always carried out in the same way, i.e. with all the individual behaviours expressed in the same order. It is also a social occasion. It can only be done in litter that is sufficiently fine, such as sand or peat. Wood shavings and straw are not suitable. A dust bath also makes financial sense: good plumage is good for the hen and saves you money on feed. In a cage system, however, special facilities need to be provided, which pushes up the cost.

Phases in dust bath behaviour
1. Preparation: the chicken raises her feathers and sits down.
2. Ruffling feathers: the chicken scratches up the sand around her so that it falls among the raised feathers. This is repeated a few times.
3. Wriggling: the chicken lies on her side and twists from side to side. Sometimes she ruffles her feathers again.
4. Shaking out: the chicken stands up, opens out her feathers and gives her body and wings a powerful shake.

A dust bath is only effective when all of these phases have been completed. If you can see that the chickens are getting no further than phases 1 and 2, then there is not enough fine litter. It is also possible that the chickens are being disturbed.

The hen ruffles her feathers to get the litter right inside.

Then she lets the litter in the feathers do its work.

Anatomy

When you talk to your advisor or vet, try to use the correct terminology to avoid confusion. To be able to observe irregularities, you first need to be able to recognise a normal bird.

1	beak	11	breast
2	nostrils	12	wing
3	comb	13	preen gland
4	ear	14	tail
5	earlobe	15	vent
6	wattles	16	stomach
7	hackle	17	shank
8	neck	18	footpad
9	back	19	claw
10	shoulder	20	nail

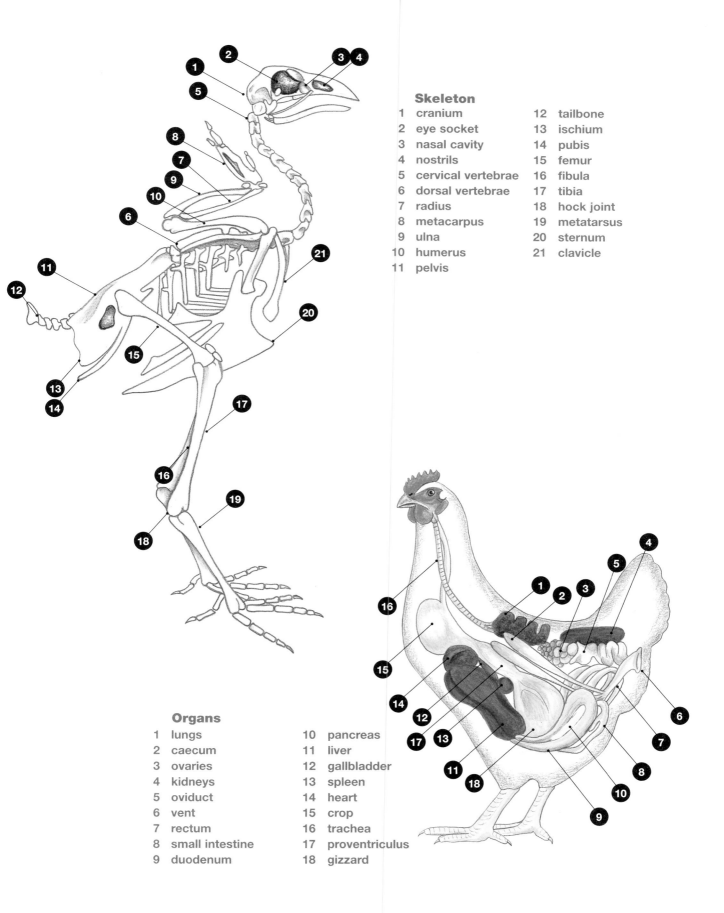

Skeleton

1	cranium	12	tailbone
2	eye socket	13	ischium
3	nasal cavity	14	pubis
4	nostrils	15	femur
5	cervical vertebrae	16	fibula
6	dorsal vertebrae	17	tibia
7	radius	18	hock joint
8	metacarpus	19	metatarsus
9	ulna	20	sternum
10	humerus	21	clavicle
11	pelvis		

Organs

1	lungs	10	pancreas
2	caecum	11	liver
3	ovaries	12	gallbladder
4	kidneys	13	spleen
5	oviduct	14	heart
6	vent	15	crop
7	rectum	16	trachea
8	small intestine	17	proventriculus
9	duodenum	18	gizzard

Senses

Most of a chicken's senses work differently from those of humans. Its eyesight is much better developed, for example, but its hearing possibly less so. There may well be other things that we humans cannot detect which a chicken can, such as the earth's magnetic field.

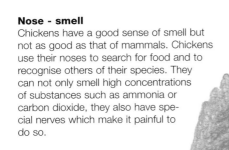

Nose - smell

Chickens have a good sense of smell but not as good as that of mammals. Chickens use their noses to search for food and to recognise others of their species. They can not only smell high concentrations of substances such as ammonia or carbon dioxide, they also have special nerves which make it painful to do so.

Eyes - sight

Chickens can see many more details and more colours and make more observations per second than we can, such as fluorescent lights (105 Hz) flickering. Chickens can see ultraviolet light and are more sensitive to other colours than we are. What we experience as white light can be light-blue or red to a hen, depending on the light source.

Tongue - taste

Chickens taste with taste buds. A chicken has 350 at most, a human 9,000. Like humans, chickens can distinguish sweet, salty, sour and bitter, but they don't like the same tastes as humans.

Beak - touch

Chickens can distinguish several contrasts with their beaks: hard/soft, hot/cold, structural differences (rough/smooth) and pain. The tip is the most sensitive part of the beak. Trimming or clipping beaks therefore causes them pain.

Ears - hearing

Chickens perceive sounds from 15 to 10,000 Hz. The human ear can hear sounds up to 20,000 Hz and can therefore hear slightly higher tones than a chicken. The sounds a chicken makes are between 400 and 6,000 Hz.

Soil and air-borne vibrations

With sensory organs in the feet and to a lesser extent in the skin, chickens are able to feel vibrations in the ground and in the air. This enables them to detect prowling predators in the dark.

Field of vision

Chickens have panoramic vision of about 300°, but the overlap between the two eyes is minimal. They can only see depth in a narrow angle (shown in green). When you go into a poultry house, you may sometimes see all the chickens briefly shaking their heads at the same time. This probably enables them to see what is happening better (with depth).

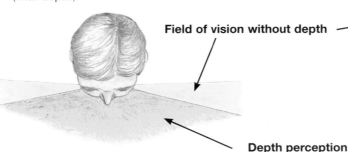

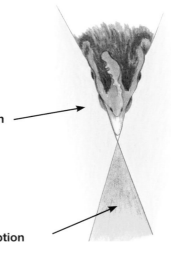

Field of vision without depth

Depth perception

Chicken sounds

Thirty different chicken sounds have been identified. Here is a description of some of their repertoire.

Being able to identify sounds enables you to pick up a number of signals. It helps put your mind at rest or identify problems early on. Unusual sounds like sniffling are often a sign of illness.

Clucking/singing

A chicken clucks when it wants or needs something, for example, just before laying, in expectation of food and when the door is opened. Excessive clucking is a sign of frustration.

Cackle

Chickens make a soft alarm cackle when danger persists. Once the danger recedes, they produce a louder cackle. The loud cackle is sometimes heard among hens that have finished laying and are coming out of the nest.

Cry of fear

A chicken may screech loudly when she is picked up. She may keep on screeching until you put her down.

Cry of pain

The cry of pain sounds like the alarm cry, but it is not as loud. It can be heard when a chicken is picked up or when a feather is pulled out. It will usually only be one cry.

Keep away from me!

Chickens have different sounds for a number of situations which all mean 'keep away from me' or 'get out of my way', for example if they are pushed aside on the roost, if they want to get rid of an intrusive rooster or when somebody comes into the nest or approaches the dust bath pit.

Alarm calls

There are different sounds for dangers in the air or on the ground, but also for the severity of the threat. A dove is announced differently from a buzzard, and a buzzard differently from a fox.

Cooing

Chickens coo just before they go to sleep if they think they can still hear or see something.

Young chicks also make different sounds. The most recognisable is the loud cheep that indicates that there is something wrong, the chick is too cold or, in natural surrounds, it has lost its mother.

The crowing of a rooster has various meanings. It is a courting or battle cry, it is used to protect its territory and it sometimes means 'watch out, rooster about' or 'I'm still here' after suffering a defeat.

Checking individual birds

Make sure you keep your finger on the pulse when you do your inspections, for example by picking up 20 hens every week and assessing them for possible problems. Take hens from different parts of the poultry house, and if you have cages, from different rows. You don't need to check for everything all the time, but train yourself by checking more and more aspects each time. Make a note of things that catch your eye so that you can check whether they are still the same next time.

Other points to check

- **Posture.** The chicken should stand tall. Chickens that are huddled up are unwell. If a chicken stands on one foot for a long time, she could be suffering from stomach pain.
- **Feet.** Smooth, shiny scales are good, but noticeably dry scales are a sign of general dehydration.
- **Comb and lobes.** A healthy comb stands upright and is a nice red colour. There should also be a red rim around the eyes.
- **Eyes.** Sagging eyelids or moist eyes are an indication of inflammation of the airways.
- **Nose and sinuses.** A dirty, wet nose and swollen sinuses indicate infections of the airways.
- **Breastbone.** Breaks are caused by accidents. Soft breastbones are either the result of insufficient calcium, phosphorus or vitamin D in the feed or poor uptake in the intestine.

When you pick up a chicken, a healthy one will offer some resistance; you'll feel the strength in the wings.

A sharply protruding bone or a bone with too little flesh indicates a lack of protein intake. The breast bone must be nice and straight.

If you hear abnormal sounds, look for wet noses and check the throat for mucus or other signs of inflammation.

Swellings or scabs on the footpads of the feet are a sign of wet or sharp litter or sharp protrusions.

Stiff or hot joints may well be inflamed.

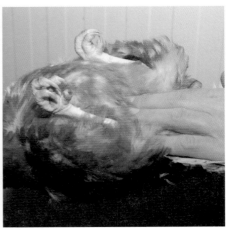

Check that the vent is moist. If the space between the leg bones is narrower than two fingers, the chicken is not laying. A good layer's leg bones can be moved smoothly and the distance between them is more than two fingers.

Weight and uniformity

Weight, and particularly fleshiness, are an indication if something is wrong with the hen's condition. Uniformity - in terms of weight differences but also in egg size – is a benchmark for the quality of your management. In other words, whether you are managing to provide all your birds - at the front and back of the poultry house, underneath and on top, and higher and lower ranking birds - with sufficient feed of the right quality. Check the fleshiness of all your birds. If there are chickens in particular places in the poultry house, such as at the bottom of the house, check that they are getting enough feed. Pay attention: something else could be wrong. Weigh the hens, preferably with an automatic weighing scale, so you can see whether anything is changing on a daily basis.

Subtle signals of disease

If animals are seriously ill, you'll notice the symptoms immediately. However, there are some diseases such as infectious bronchitis which you can't identify immediately just by looking at the animals. You will see lower levels of feed and water intake, or you will notice that the shell colour of the eggs has changed or the eggs show defects. If the chickens start laying fewer eggs or laying later in the day, then there has been a problem for a while. This is a sign that there is something wrong and that you have missed something.

The weighing scale in this cage is in the shape of a short perch which the chickens are happy to sit on.

In cage systems with tiers at different heights, the temperature is higher at the top than at the bottom. The hens in the bottom cages will need extra maintenance feed per day. Rule of thumb: each chicken needs one gram of extra food per day for every degree of lower temperature.

Manure

Chickens produce two types of manure: intestinal and caecal. Intestinal faeces are solid with a white cap of urates. Caecal droppings are more of a shiny, firm paste, dark-green to brown in colour. The manure is not right if it is milky white, green, yellow or orange or if it contains blood. The manure is also not right if it is not firm enough, too wet, foamy or poorly digested (feed-coloured or still containing feed components).

Intestinal faeces

Caecal droppings

CHAPTER 2

The chicken and her environment

Cage or floor: there is a world of difference between the two. With caged chickens, it's mainly the farmer who calls the shots. In non-caged systems the hens determine what happens and you, the poultry farmer, have to respond accordingly. You can control their behaviour with food, water, light and other factors.

Good management requires thinking about things from the hen's point of view and looking out for them properly.

Ideal home

The chicken prefers her living environment to be divided up so that there is a separate area for each activity: resting, laying eggs, scratching, eating and drinking, dust bathing. For resting, laying eggs and dust baths she needs quiet places where she won't be disturbed by other chickens coming and going.

A healthy living environment naturally also includes the right temperature and the right amount of light, air, food and water.

These perches are at the top of the house where there are no other facilities. The resting chickens are not disturbed there, so they can get real peace and quiet.

Choosing a system that works for you

The choice of a husbandry system is not a purely financial one. There are many other factors involved, such as how much time you have and what sort of jobs you like to do. There is no unequivocally 'good' or 'bad' system. Compare the various systems and consider the objective pros and cons of each one, but also think about what you yourself regard as pros and cons.

Downsides of switching to alternative

1. Floor eggs
2. Dehydrated hens
3. Hens that start moulting from a lack of feed and water
4. When something goes wrong the consequences are more serious. With an alternative system, an infection can spread through the entire poultry house more quickly, for example.

Driving licence

'If keeping caged chickens is like cycling, keeping chickens in a floor system is like driving a car, and keeping aviary chickens is like driving a lorry. You need a pilot's licence to keep organic chickens.'

A poultry farmer

Points to consider with non-caged systems

- As a poultry farmer you have less leisure time because the work is less easy to delegate to others
- When something goes wrong the consequences are more serious
- You must be more aware of the behaviour of your birds and know how to respond to it
- You must spend more time in the poultry house with the hens, so it is more hands-on
- The laying phase must follow on seamlessly from the rearing phase; consult your supplier about this.
- Ventilation systems work differently in non-caged housing:
  - fewer chickens, so less heat is generated
  - more sensitive to weather influences
  - with a range, ventilation based on underpressure is not possible.

Infections spread faster in a house with non-caged chickens than in a caged system because the chickens spread the germs all over the house.

Differences between husbandry systems

This table is of course mainly theoretical. As a poultry farmer you must also be committed to a particular method of keeping chickens. If you keep chickens in an alternative system without really believing in it, you are asking for trouble.

	Cage/ enriched cage	Colony housing	Traditional floor system	Aviary	Free- range	Organic
Cost price	++	++	+/-	+	-	- -
Labour	++	+	+/-	+/-	-	-
Operational safety	+/-	++	+	+	+/-	+ / -
Leisure time	++	++	+	+/-	-	-
Animal health	+	+	+/-	+/-	-	-
Dust	+	+	- -	- -	- -	- -
Ammonia in house	+	+	-	+/-	-	-
Food safety	++	++	+/-	+/-	-	-
Natural behaviour	- -	-	+	+	++	++
Image	- -	-	+	+	++	++

Rating: ++ very good, + good, +/- average, - poor, -- very poor

Moving in

Moving to a new home is very disruptive for the birds, so it is important to do all you can to help them settle in quickly. Think of it like friends coming to visit: you would also offer them a nice cup of tea and a biscuit in a comfortable room. The same applies to how you welcome your new hens. After a long journey they are arriving at their new home. Make it quiet and comfortable.

For example, make sure they can find everything easily and that the temperature is right. The better you do this, the more likely you are to have a good cycle and the less likely you are to have problems. In effect, you are simply continuing to rear the birds. You only become a laying hen farmer when the first egg is laid; until then you are a rearer - just as a woman only becomes a mother when she has her first baby.

18°C is a comfortable poultry house temperature. Warm up the poultry house if necessary before the hens arrive. After all, the hens have not eaten for a while and will get cold more quickly, risking getting off to a poor start.

The drinking water system in the rearing poultry house must be similar to the system in the laying poultry house. If you have a nipple drinking system, Make sure the drip is visible so the birds recognise it as a water source. The colour of the nipple might play a role as well, so you could also use some nipple in the 'rearing colour'.

Perches

Chickens naturally like to rest and sleep high up to keep out of the reach of predators. In addition, conflicts between hens are resolved sooner if the hens can take refuge on perches. This makes for a calmer environment. A minimum of 15 cm of perch length per hen is required by law (or 18 cm on organic farms). Perches made of plastic or metal are very hard-wearing and stay very clean. Wooden perches soon get soiled with manure and are a breeding ground for red mites.

Positioning the perches

Perches in cages must not get in the way or prevent the hens from walking on the slats. Perches must be at least 6 cm above the slats to allow eggs to roll under them.

The top perches fill up first: if they don't, you have a housing problem.

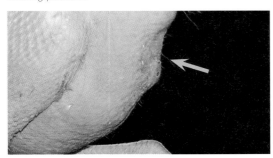

Older chickens can suffer from a softening of the breastbone. The breastbone also becomes porous as a result of calcium, phosphorus or vitamin D3 deficiency. Under these circumstances sitting on a perch can cause the breastbone to become deformed.

Right: rounded top edges and enough width to support the toes.

Right: round edges and enough width to support the toes.

Wrong: a round profile is difficult to grip. It's also too thin, so it provides insufficient support and encourages extra nail growth.

Wrong: too thin, so there is no support for the toes.

Wrong: too thin, so there is not enough support for the toes.

Not all perches are appropriate. The best shape is flat on top with rounded edges. This gives the chicken a good grip.

LOOK-THINK-ACT

A night light for chickens?

This photograph shows a dark aviary house with only the system lights on. This is a good way of enticing the hens into the system for the night. You can do this in two ways: firstly by using dimmable lighting, and secondly by switching off the lights in groups, from the bottom to the top of the system and finally the lure lights at the very top. Make sure these lights are above the resting places so that they actually lure the chickens onto the perches. You don't want all the hens to move up to the lamps, so don't leave them on too long.

Litter

Chickens have two basic needs for which they need litter: scratching and dust bathing. For a chicken, scratching (scraping with the feet) is inextricably linked to eating. Dust baths are for keeping the feathers clean and free of parasites. Dust baths reduce the risk of feathers becoming brittle and breaking, so the plumage remains in good condition for longer. This also keeps your feed bill down. Wood shavings and straw are good for scratching in, but smaller particles such as sand are needed for a dust bath.

Keeping nails trim

In non-caged systems nails stay short as the hens scratch through the litter and scrabble across the concrete floor. In cages, chickens can only keep their nails short by providing special facilities like abrasive strips on the egg protection panel which the hens scrabble across while feeding. This abrasive material is compulsory in cages. Materials that meet this requirement include scouring pastes, hard metal strips with a rough surface and stone abrasive strips. Perforated egg protection panels are slightly less effective and are actually only used for brown hens as the nails on brown hens grow more slowly. Adhesive strips are cheap but they generally do not last more than one laying cycle.

The nails of these chickens are too long. Fit new abrasive strips.

Bath time bliss

This photograph shows hens on a litter mat in a colony cage. They are very busy with the litter that has just been provided. To make the litter mat more suitable for dust baths, the litter is deposited on the mat from the pipe at the back of the cage. This should ideally be done several times a day. An additional benefit is that this also reduces the risk of feather pecking.

These birds have litter, but if the flock is large or there are a lot of feather peckers, their dust bath behaviour is interrupted too often, so they don't get the full benefit of the dust baths.

Clean and dry

Store packaged products such as wood shavings and chopped straw indoors or under cover and on pallets to prevent the litter from getting wet. Avoid damaging the packaging; this will reduce the risk of contamination and vermin.

Wood fibre delivered loose must be stored in a dry place. Cover it with breathable cloth to prevent contamination by wild birds and mould formation from condensation. Vermin control is essential in all cases.

A bale of straw or alfalfa gives chickens the chance to peck and scratch. They pull the bale to pieces.

Pros and cons of litter material for laying hens

Litter material	Dust formation	Availability	Poultry health	Dust bath	Moisture uptake
Wood shavings [1]	-	+/-	+/-	+	++
Sawdust [1]	- -	+/-	Risk of crop blockage	+	+
Chopped Wheat straw [2]	-	++	+/-	-	+
Chopped rape seed straw [2]	-	++	+/-	-	++
Maize silage [2]	+	++	Good for intestinal health on account of acidity level. Reduces footpad lesions	+	+/-
Peat [3]	--	-	Reduces footpad lesions. Risk of crop blockage	++	++
Alfalfa	+	+	Positive effect of raw fibres on intestinal health	++	--
Sand [4]	+	++	Improves gizzard function. Risk of contamination with pathogens	-	+/-

++ very positive, + positive, +/- average, - negative, -- very negative

[1] Availability of wood products has declined in recent years and is seasonal. Supply is limited during the winter months.
[2] These products can contain mould spores. Greater risk of mould formation if stored inappropriately or in damp places in the house. Straw and maize in poultry manure are better for the soil than wood products, despite the risk of weed seeds.
[3] Peat is extracted in countries like Scandinavia and the Balkans; may contain high concentrations of heavy metals.
[4] If chickens eat too much sand, this can cause problems in the abattoir and with manure incineration.

Climate under control

The climate in a house is a combination of temperature, air velocity, indoor air composition, dust and light. These factors can impact on one another. Get a climate expert to check both the climate computer and the climate once or preferably twice per year. The expert works with these systems every day and knows what the best setting should be. Sometimes it will be different from the manufacturer's recommended setting. The expert can also pick up on changes in the sensors which could indicate that the climate is no longer being optimally controlled. Naturally you should also be alert to signals that indicate whether or not the climate is right. Chickens might avoid certain places or crawl on top of each other, for example, or there may be a musty smell. You get used to bad air quite quickly, so go with the impression you get when you enter the house.

When setting the house temperature, take the quality of the plumage into account. A featherless hen needs a higher temperature.

Air flow in an aviary house

Wrong

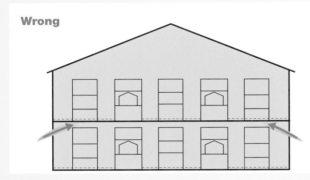

Bad air circulation can occur in houses containing a small number of chickens and a relatively large number of obstacles. Air does not circulate properly in aviary houses that are too low. There are also 'dead corners' in the middle of the house.

Right

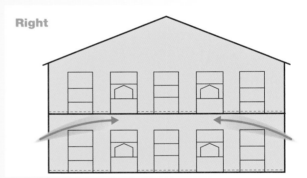

There is plenty of room above the tiers to allow the air right into the middle of the house. There is therefore less of a risk of 'dead corners'. You can also direct air to the middle of the house with pipes or ducts from outside running along the ceiling to the middle.

LOOK-THINK-ACT

What is wrong with this temperature sensor?

This temperature sensor is level with the top perch. That's too high. For accurate temperature measurement, it is important that the temperature sensors register the temperature where the chickens are. So it must be in among the chickens, but not in a position where the chickens can sit against it. Check regularly that the temperature sensors are working properly by hanging a good manual thermometer next to them.

Skin temperature (wind chill factor)

As it becomes warmer outdoors, poor ventilation can cause the house to become musty. This is one of the causes of feather pecking. So you will need to ventilate the house well, ensure a good air velocity and monitor the temperature. Make sure the set minimum ventilation is appropriate to the number of hens, and assume 0.7 m3/kg live weight per hour. Ventilation-directed air flow has a cooling effect on the hens, because the wind chill factor increases as the air velocity increases. Watch out for draughts. Hens will avoid draughty places. The optimum skin temperature for hens in cages is 20 to 24°C. For hens in non-caged systems it is 18 to 22°C. Higher temperatures over long periods of time, particularly above 28 to 30°C, combined with high relative humidity can lead to heat stress. In case of acute heat stress, hens sit with their beaks open and their wings spread out. This causes higher mortality and a drop in production. Chronic heat stress has more gradual effects.

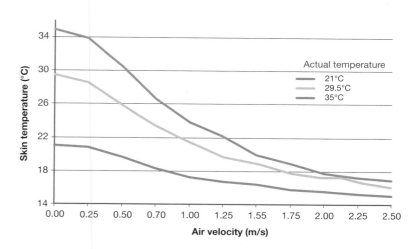

The temperature the chickens experience depends on the combination of outside temperature, relative humidity and air velocity. Higher air velocities in high outside temperatures can create a strong cooling effect. But watch out for draughts.

Wind: not too little, not too much

One disadvantage of natural ventilation is that there is virtually no ventilation when there is no wind. Use auxiliary fans to ensure sufficient air circulation. Fresh air can also reach the birds via the aeration of the manure conveyors.

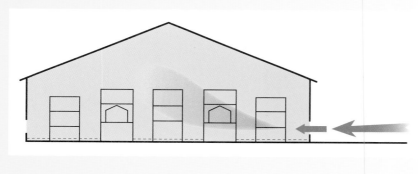

In houses with natural ventilation, the wind affects the interior climate. Too high air velocities can create draughts, and draughts can also pop up at different places in the house.

An evergreen windbreak or vertical walls outside the range openings around the house is one way of reducing the effects of wind.

Air

High ammonia and dust levels affect the chickens' mucous membranes and make them more sus-ceptible to disease. In fact, too much ammonia causes blindness in chickens. You can smell ammonia from a concentration of as little as 20 ppm yourself. If you can smell it, the concentration is too high. Other gases like oxygen, carbon dioxide and carbon monoxide have no smell. Imperceptible to humans, excessive concentrations can be harmful to the birds, but also to humans. Ventilation not only brings fresh air into the house, it also removes residues in the air.

If you have several poultry houses, you may sometimes notice the hens in different houses doing different things. If the birds in one house are less active than those in another, this may well have something to do with the climate. Monitor it, or get someone in to do so, and improve your ventilation system if necessary. You can monitor most gases easily yourself using gas detection tubes. The table gives the standard levels for the main gases.

Avoid wet litter

Wet litter is a source of ammonia and leads more quickly to digestive problems, coccidiosis and footpad problems (lameness). Keep the litter dryer by ventilating better (removing the moisture), increasing the fibre content in the feed (result: dryer manure) and stopping spillages of drinking water. Scatter grain so that the hens scratch the litter loose themselves.

Concentrations of various gases

Gas	Standard level
Oxygen (O_2)	> 21%
Carbon dioxide (CO_2)	< 0.2% (2000 ppm)
Carbon monoxide (CO)	< 0.01% (100 ppm) (ideally 0)
Ammonia (NH_3)	< 0.002% (20 ppm)
Hydrogen sulphide (H_2S)	< 0.002% (20 ppm)
Relative humidity	60-70%

You can see that the litter in this picture has become a hard crust. The litter was originally damp and was obviously not worked enough by the chickens.

When you monitor the house climate, don't only do so at your own working height but also at the height of the chickens.

Light

A properly lit house gives you a good overall view of the house and your hens. By distributing light throughout the space and over time, you can influence where the birds go and when, and whether they are active or rest. Day length and light intensity influence feed consumption and production.

Did you know that a chicken...

- sees more colours than humans in daylight?
- sees the light of conventional fluorescent tubes as flickering? This does not apply to high-frequency lamps, which are also more economical to run.
- prefer at least 60 lux for eating, drinking and scratching?
- prefer semi-darkness for egg laying and roosting: 0.5 to 1 lux?
- recognise others of their species better in more intensive light (> 70 lux)?

Pros and cons of lighting systems

	Incan-descent lamp	High-frequency fluorescent tube	Orion PL lamp*	SL-lamp	High-pressure sodium vapour lamp
Purchase price	+	--	-	+/-	+/-
Installation costs	-	+	-	-	++
Peripherals	+/-	+/-	+/-	+/-	+/-
Maintenance costs	+/-	+	+	+	+
Power consumption	--	++	++	++	++
Service life	--	+	+	+	++
Dimming	++	++	+	-	+/-
Light distribution	++	+	++	+	-
Spectrum display	+	+/-	--	-	--
Stroboscopic effect	++	++	++	--	+
Feather pecking/ cannibalism	+	+	++	--	+/-

++ = very good; + = good; +/- = average; - = poor; -- = very poor
* In laying hen houses with the Orion PL system, one half consists of red lamps and the other half of white ones.

LOOK-THINK-ACT

Dark spots?

There are dark spots in some places under the racks in this aviary house. The hens will want to lay their eggs there. If you want to avoid floor eggs there, fit rope lights as shown in this picture.

Dust

There's no such thing as a dust-free house. Litter, manure, feed and feathers all turn into dust eventually. Dust is bad for the health of the hens and the poultry farmer. Dust particles get into the lungs. In combination with ammonia, which affects the mucous membranes, this increases the risk of infection in the birds. Breathing in dust is also dangerous to human health, particularly:

- in high concentrations
- when you stay in the house for a long time
- with very fine particles.

What starts out as a seemingly harmless symptom like a tickle at the back of your throat, sneezing and coughing can turn into serious illnesses like bronchitis, shortness of breath, asthma or reduced lung capacity.

Never underestimate the health risks of dust; always wear a dust mask. The amount of particulates in the air is also governed by ever stricter EU regulations which you will need to take into account.

Types of dust

The smaller the dust particles, the deeper they penetrate into the lungs and the more harmful they are.

They are classified as follows:

- Inhalable dust: particles of less than 50-100 µm. You can inhale these particles, but you can also expel them via the cilia in the lungs.
- Thoracic dust or particulate: particles of less than 10 µm.
- Respirable dust: particles less than 4 µm. These are very small particles that come to rest in the alveoli and damage the lung function.

Dirt and dust in inlet valves and ventilation ducts cause more resistance. This reduces the ventilation capacity, so the temperature rises. The electricity consumption will rise unnecessarily.

Keeping the aisles in a house with cages clean helps to cut down on dust. Cleaning weekly prevents large amounts of dust from settling which can be disturbed again. Tip: Use a clean filter. An ineffective or old filter will cause the vacuum cleaner to re-expel some of the dust particles. So clean and replace the filter regularly. And don't forget to wear a dust mask yourself.

A lot of dust is released during vaccination. When doing these kinds of tasks, always wear a dust mask. Correct use of a dust mask reduces the risk of inhaling dust by 90%. Masks with an exhalation valve are more comfortable to wear. Use P2 masks as a very minimum.

Solutions for the future

1. Applying an oil film: binding dust particles by applying a film of rapeseed oil or sunflower oil over the litter. This reduces the amount of dust by 50-90%. Downside: dirt becomes caked.

2. Water spray: settle dust by spraying with clean water. This reduces the amount of dust by 80% (coarse dust) and 50% (fine dust). Downsides: Relative humidity in the house can become too high, so the litter can get too wet.

3. Air recirculation with cleaning: outgoing air can be recirculated after cleaning (e.g. filtration, air washing). This reduces the amount of dust by 40-60%.

4. Ionisation: settle the dust by charging the dust particles by applying a voltage difference. The charged particles will then stick to earthed surfaces like the floor and walls. This reduces the amount of dust by about 35%.

These techniques have an additional environmental benefit: much less dust is emitted into the open air.

Spraying the litter with oil

Ionisation: there is a voltage difference along the wire with protrusions.

Activities and their dust scores

Presence between hens	Dust score
Delivery of layers	12
Removing birds (catching and loading)	12
Handling individual birds (healthcare etc.)	12
Collecting floor eggs in aviary and floor systems	12
Treating groups of hens (group vaccination)	6
Inspections among birds	3
Delivery of broilers	2

Other activities in the house	
Cleaning the house	12
Removing dust from aisles, dry	12
Removing dust from aisles, wet	8
Scattering straw and litter	6
Mucking out chicken house with shovel/loader	6
Collecting eggs and inspecting in lobby	4
Inspecting from feed aisle during feeding in cage systems	3
Inspecting from feed aisle outside feeding times in cage systems	2

The dust burden in the house varies depending on the activity. The dust score ranges from 1 to 18, with 18 indicating a very high dust burden and 1 a very low one. These figures do not represent the absolute quantities of dust but a combination of quantity and time. For example, removing hens generates a lot of dust but only for a short period; floor eggs generate very little dust but over a longer period. So the total dust burden of these two activities is the same.

www.pakstofaan.nl

Home on the range

An outdoor range can make a significant contribution to the well-being of your birds. Chickens that get outdoors are less likely to feather-peck. But you need to make the range attractive for the birds and keep it properly maintained.

The ideal range?

A chicken range will meet both people's and birds' expectations if it gives the poultry farmer a good view of the flock, provides enough shelter for the chickens and looks green and well cared for as well. The chickens should feel safe in it and should be able to spread out over the whole of the available space. Chickens are descended from woodland birds, so they need plenty of shelter. On the other hand, the poultry farmer needs to have a clear view of the birds, so the range should not be too densely planted. The range should be practical to maintain. The amount of work needs to be manageable, preferably using the poultry farm's existing machinery rather than having to hire in specialist contractors. And finally, the range is the farm's calling card for the general public. Yet another reason why the range should be kept neat and tidy. Members of the public expect to see lots of green: neatly mown and trimmed and blending in well with the landscape.

There is a gutter under the slats. The chickens cross the slats before they go into the house, so they carry less mud inside on their feet. Discharge the gutter into the manure tank.

In a system with a well-designed range, chickens can indulge in their natural behaviour to the full.

The facts

Is a range good for welfare and production? This question is difficult to answer if you are talking about all birds on all free-range farms as a whole. This is because it is not just the presence of a range that impacts on welfare, health and production, but also how it is designed and maintained, whether the hens like using it and how consistently the poultry farmer lets his hens out.

Positive effects on animal welfare

- Birds can express more behaviours outdoors (sunbathing, running around, searching for food).

- Free-range chickens are less nervous than indoor ones because they are used to more stimuli.

- Chickens that go outdoors a lot have better plumage than chickens that rarely if ever go outdoors.

- Fat liver is less common in free-range chickens.

Negative effects on animal welfare

- Free-range chickens are more susceptible to attacks by predators.

- Losses are higher on average among free-range chickens.

- Free-range chickens are more susceptible to health problems like worms, blackhead, Erysipelas, Pasteurela and Coccidiosis.

Impact on bird performance

- Depending on the breed, free-range chickens can be as productive as indoor chickens.

- Eggs from free-range chickens often have stronger shells.

- Eggs from free-range chickens may contain more dioxins.

- Eggs from free-range chickens may be lighter in colour.

- Free-range chickens need more feed with a higher energy content because they move around more and are exposed to greater differences in temperature.

How do you get them outdoors?

First time outdoors on a laying farm

As soon as the chickens know where to find food and water in the house, they can go outdoors (after 1-2 days). You don't need to keep them indoors for weeks on end until they are laying properly or are used to the nests. If you keep them indoors in the mornings, they will have plenty of time to get used to the nests.

More light in the house

If the house is dark, there will be a big difference between indoors and outdoors, so the hens will be less inclined to go outdoors. Increase the lighting in the house, preferably with daylight, even though it loses some of its quality when it passes through glass or transparent corrugated panels (the UV light is filtered out). A covered range can also help them get used to the change in light levels.

Treats at the back

To get the chickens right to the back (and keep them there), you will have to offer them something that is not available everywhere, such as drinking towers and shelter. Because it stays dry under the side roofs, they are a good place for sand baths. Although feeding in the range is not encouraged, you can offer mown grass, fodder beet, a strip of sown grain, sunflowers or other edible crops to entice the chickens out.

Down the line

To get the chickens away from the house, you can arrange linear elements in the range. The chickens will run along them to the end and spread out better.

The chickens don't mind what you put there, as long as there is something.

You can even put tree stumps in a line leading away from the house.

LOOK-THINK-ACT

Why aren't my chickens going outdoors?

There are several possible explanations. The range is quite bare so there is no shelter. The hens feel insecure outside. There could be a strong current of air blowing through the hatches into the house. The chickens have to go 'against the wind' to get outside. Remedy this by reducing the underpressure in the house: open the intake flaps or valves as well as the inlet openings. More shelter in the range or even a covered veranda could encourage the hens to go outdoors.

Gimme shelter

Chickens only feel safe when there is shelter near-by. This can take the form of natural vegetation or an artificial shelter. What is important is that the hens can stand under or next to it. It is not only shelter inside the range itself that makes them feel safe; a wooded bank immediately alongside will also do the trick. There must be some form of shelter within 10 to 15 metres of every point in the range, so that if chickens get frightened by something they don't have to run indoors. Chickens that only feel safe indoors will hardly ever go outdoors. The presence of roosters can also help.

Willows are easy to propagate. From mid-November to early March, take one-year-old shoots or a thick branch and plant them in a hole that reaches the groundwater. Removing the bark from the bottom part encourages even more root growth.

You can sometimes get grants to buy saplings for planting up woodland areas.

Make the range multifunctional: use it as a vineyard, for example. The vines provide shelter and are high enough not to be a temptation to hungry chickens. The fact that there are people pruning and harvesting in the range on a regular basis makes it even more attractive for the chickens.

In this range, trees are being trained to form natural parasols. In a few years the trees will have a full crown. Training the branches horizontally creates a tree shape that provides shelter in winter too.

Artificial shelter

Camouflage nets (left) disintegrate if they are left out in the open the whole year round, but are a good temporary solution when the maize has been harvested or other forms of shelter are not yet fully operational.

The shelter on this farm (right) is portable. The chickens use it as a refuge when they take fright.

Bad behaviour and problematic pests

If you don't maintain the range, the chickens will strip it bare and you will be left with a compacted topsoil layer which won't absorb rainwater properly. This can give rise to damp, especially round the house. How to prevent damp:

- Make sure the ground is sloping so that rainwater drains away and does not need to soak into the ground.
- Concrete around the house to make the most susceptible part easier to keep clean.
- Lay gravel or rubble around the outside of the house with drainage below.
- Pave around the outside of the house and fit a gutter.
- Loosen the soil with a cultivator as soon as you notice puddles starting to form.
- Scatter wood chippings or tree bark.
- Plant willows or other trees that draw water from the soil.

Foxes

If you have a problem with foxes, lay the bottom half metre of the fence flat along the ground pointing away from the range and fit an electric wire along the top. When a fox tries to get under the fence, it can't get past the wire netting. If it wants to jump over the fence, it is stopped by the electric wire.

There will always be some chickens that manage to escape from the range. Fortunately there are also some handy ways of dealing with this. Make holes in the fences in strategic places and make one-way gates out of thick metal wire. The chickens can get in but they can't get back out (not applicable in case you have a fox around).

LOOK-THINK-ACT

Not all my chickens go back inside in the evening. What should I do?

Some of the chickens are spending the night in the trees on the far side. This is because there is no shelter in the middle of the range which the chickens can run along to get back to the house. Install linear elements and fit an outside light near the house. Switch off the light when the last chicken has got to the house and before the lights are switched off inside. The light inside and the herding instinct will make the chickens go indoors.

Covered range or winter garden

It's often not possible or feasible to provide a real outdoor range. In that case, consider providing a covered range, also known as a winter garden or cold scratching area. The benefits for the birds are that there is daylight, a different temperature zone and some diversion. This space also counts towards your house area, so you can keep more birds. You can also use the winter garden to provide the chickens with a diversion:

- bales of lucerne hay
- freshly mown grass
- barrels of normal grit or gizzard grit
- perches
- containers of sand.

Right: On this farm, a strip of grass is mown every day and fed to the chickens.

Wrong: There is a lot of daylight in this covered range, which makes the chickens active. But there isn't even any litter to scratch in, so the chickens start feather pecking out of boredom. Inset: The same farm a few months later: lots of bald hens.

Right: In this covered range, trees have been planted which will provide shade in the future. Drinking water is also available.

New housing systems are increasingly designed around the hens' natural needs. This takes more understanding of animal behaviour by the farmer. And a lot of attention and focused action to get all the hens to lay in the nests.

CHAPTER 3

Rearing hens

The rearing of pullets is geared towards supplying hens that are healthy and problem-free and that will supply the poultry farmer with lots of good quality eggs.

The circumstances during rearing account for 60-70 per cent of the birds' technical performance on the laying farm.

As a rearer it is in your interest to ensure that the hens develop properly and uniformly. If you use alternative systems, you will also need to teach the hens to move through the house properly so that they go into the laying house to look for feed, water and a laying nest.

A rearing cycle is successful when the hens are uniform, have a good weight on delivery and get off to a flying start on the laying farm, assuming that the poultry farmer looks after them well on arrival.

By the time they reach the rearing farm, the chickens will already have gone through quite a lot: all the handling at the hatchery, transportation, a new environment and changing climatic conditions.

The early days

Day-old chicks must be handled with care, and there are a number of basic things to bear in mind. A flock that gets off to a good start is easier to control, has a higher body weight at the start of the rearing process, is more uniform, has a better health status and reaches 'genetic potential' more easily.

Before the chicks arrive, **check** that everything in the house is working properly: heating, thermostats, ventilation, feed and water system (water pressure on the nipples, no residues or disinfectants in the water) and lighting. It is also important to make sure the water is microbiologically clean. Because of the high temperature in the house, you will need to change the water one day before the chicks arrive.

Depending on the outside temperature, **heat the house** 24 to 48 hours before the chicks arrive or build it up to the right temperature for the chicks over four days (20°, 25°, 28°, 30° and on arrival 38°C). It is not just the air that needs to be at the right temperature but the whole inventory: the slats, the paper, the feeding system and the drinking water. Cold water (< 20°C) leads to a lower body temperature, which day-old chicks can't adjust. Make sure the temperature at the level of the chicks is between 33 and 35°C. In a floor system, the temperature of the litter must be about 30°C. You can measure this with an infrared thermometer.

Check the **relative humidity** (min. 55%). In cold periods, if you need extra heat you can install a spray head on your heat cannon if necessary, or throw a couple of buckets of water over the scratching area; that will work wonders.

Keep an eye on the **carbon dioxide level**. If you ventilate too little, in cold periods for example, the carbon dioxide level can increase. If the chicks are lethargic and you get a slightly heavy head (or a headache), you probably need to ventilate more.

Make a **checklist** which you can adapt and correct each time. Then you won't forget anything important.

These five-day old chicks are all sticking their heads out of the cage. This could be because they are too hot or the carbon dioxide level in the air is too high.

LOOK-THINK-ACT

Why are these chicks all bunched up together?

They are all standing on the last piece of poultry paper. They obviously prefer standing on the paper than on the slats.
If the whole surface is slatted, cover it with thick paper, ideally with a layer of litter and feed.
Thick paper remains intact longer, so the litter and feed stay in place longer. Rather use thin paper in places that are likely to get damp, such as below the drinking lines.

Quality of day-old chicks

The quality of a day-old chick is a reflection of the condition of the parent birds and the hatching process. The chicks of young mother birds are smaller and need a higher temperature and humidity, for example. If you know your chicks' weaknesses, you can take additional steps to prevent problems.

Assess at least twenty chicks to get an impression of your flock of day-old chicks. If there are too many poor quality chicks, talk to the hatchery or rearer about what steps to take. The chicks' body temperature drops between the time when they come out of the hatching machine and the time they arrive in the house. It has been found that chicks coming off the truck at 37 degrees have a 10% loss rate during the first few days. If you are not sure about the body temperature, measure it at the vent with an ear thermometer.

Behaviour of a flock of day-old chicks

The chicks' behaviour is a key indicator that everything is as it should be. After arrival, spread out the boxes of chicks around the house and place the chicks by the feed and water. Check them every couple of hours.

- Chicks are spreading out all over the space: temperature and ventilation are fine.
- Chicks are huddling together in some places, are less active, don't start moving around and look as if they are in a daze: temperature is too low.
- Chicks are avoiding certain places: it could be draughty there.
- Chicks are lying on the ground with wings spread out, seem to be gasping for air and start to chirp: it is too hot or there is too much carbon dioxide in the air (measure=know).

(See also the chapter on Broilers).

Assessing day-old chicks individually: what to look for

Check	Right	Wrong
Reflex: Lay chick on its back	Chick should stand up within 3 seconds.	Chick takes more than 3 seconds to stand up: chick is listless
Eyes	Clean, open and shiny	Closed, dull
Navel	Navel should be closed and clean	Bumpy: remnants of yolk; open navel; feathers smeared with albumen
Feet	Feed should be a normal colour and not swollen	Red hocks, swollen hocks, malformations
Beak	Beak clean with closed nostrils	Red beak; dirty nostrils; malformations
Yolk sac	Stomach soft and malleable	Stomach hard and skin taut
Down	Should be dry and shiny	Down wet and tacky
Uniformity	All chicks the same size	More than 20% of chicks are 20% heavier or lighter than average
Temperature	Should be between 40 and 40.8°C.	Above 41.1°C: too high, below 38°C: too low. Should be 40° 2-3 hours after arrival.

Navels

Check whether there are any chicks with poorly closed navels due to the yolk sac not being fully withdrawn. These navels often do not close at all and pose a greater risk of loss. So you don't want chicks with poorly closed navels in your flock. Make a note of how many there are and discuss it with the hatchery. An open navel with no obstructions will close properly.

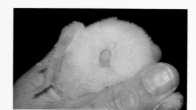
Normal: navel will close.

Abnormal: cannot close because the yolk sac is in the way.

Weight and condition

When underweight birds come into lay, this can affect their overall output. Hens that have more developed laying organs and thus a higher body weight are not a problem as long as they are not fat. Be aware that weight standards on the rearing farm are minimums and maximums of individual hens. If the average weight is around the minimum standard, you will have too many low body weight individuals. If there is a weight difference between hens in the top and bottom tiers, introduce measures that will enable them to move more easily through the system.

Calculating uniformity

Calculate uniformity at 15 weeks. Weigh 1-3% of the birds throughout the house and in various tiers. Work out the average and the percentage of birds in a bandwidth of 10% either side of the average. Uniformity of at least 80 is good, particularly in combination with a good weight.
If the uniformity is lower than 80 because there are a lot of small chicks, allow them to grow a little before starting light stimulation. If it is lower because there are a lot of large birds, you may be able to start stimulation; check with the layer farmer first.

By the end of the rearing period, the combs are larger and redder. There is also more colour round the eyes, as you can see in this photograph.

Moulting stage of wing feathers

Before egg production rearing hens moult four times: One complete moult and three times partially. A smooth moulting and proper continuation of moulting beyond 16 weeks is a healthy sign. At 15 or 16 weeks, count the number of wing feathers that have not yet moulted. When the hens only have a two feathers to go, you can start light stimulation (moulting score 2 or less). See also page 57.

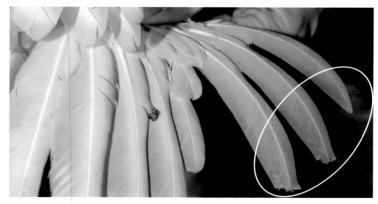

Hens moult their wing feathers from the inside out. This hen still has three feathers to moult, namely the long ones on the far right. Long, often pointed feathers are the oldest and have therefore not yet been shed.

Factors influencing uniformity:
- Number of hens per m²
- Feeding structure (selective feeding)
- Length and height of feeder
- Length of drinker (nipples) and availability of water
- Quality of beak trimming
- Stress factors (disease, vaccination)
- Age at which uniformity is measured (sexual development)
- Genetic background (breed of chicken)
- Weighing method: The more chicks you weigh, the more accurate the uniformity will be.

Automatic weighing in the house provides information about weight and uniformity.

Light

Lighting programme

Both the lighting programme and the composition of the feed affect the growth and development of the chickens. With the young chicks, start with the maximum light intensity, then you can dim it slightly if necessary. The golden rule is: Never extend the length of the day and the light intensity during rearing. Even increasing from 9 to 10 hours during rearing represents stimulation.

Rest and routine

Rest and routine are keywords in the early stages of rearing, just as with human babies. A good lighting and feeding plan helps achieve this. The birds are encouraged to eat, but they also get sufficient rest. This helps reduce mortality. Each time the light goes on, the chicks are activated to look for food and water. This helps them synchronise their behaviour and get into a good rhythm. It also makes them easier to check.

Daylight during rearing

There is no daylight in most rearing houses. If you do have daylight, it is important not to increase the day length at all during the growing period (development and maturing phase).
Establish what the natural day length is when the chicks are 18 weeks old. Then you can adjust the lighting programme to the daylight in two ways.
1. Provide additional lighting to make sure the day length from 8 weeks is the same as the natural day length at 18 weeks.
2. Using additional lighting, provide a long enough day during the growing phase to enable you to shorten the day length in the last phase so as to reach the natural day length at 18 weeks. This 'step-down system' begins at week 10.

Example of a lighting and feeding programme

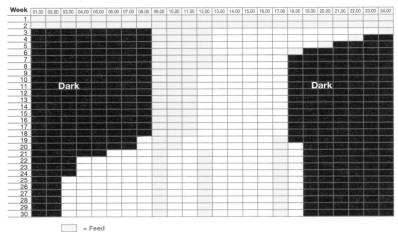

= Feed

These organic rearing hens see more and are more active in daylight than in artificial light.

Increasing feed intake

When the hens come into lay, they need to increase their feed intake in a short space of time. Prepare them for this in the rearing house. One common way of doing this is by block feeding, or feeding at set times. They will then eat more than when they are offered food continuously. Their intestines get used to a higher feed intake.

Increasing the fibre content is another method (more common in organic poultry farming). They will eat more volume to meet their nutritional requirements. Additional advantages of a higher fibre diet are: better digestion, drier litter, less ammonia, less feather pecking and better intestinal health.

Teaching good behaviour in aviaries

After layers are set up in an aviary, they find it easier to look for feed, water, laying nests and perches if they have learned to jump and look for things they need in the rearing stage. You can improve hens' mobility by training them.

In a Nivo Varia house, as the hens get older more and more levels become available. Feed and water are provided further away from each other than in an aviary.

Aviary rearing: water training

The chicks spend the first few weeks in the middle tier. Everything they need is there: feed and water. Not all chicks will leave this tier of their own accord: only the inquisitive ones will venture out. As soon as the chicks are physically able to jump, in other words when half or a third start jumping over the edge, let them go. Don't let the chicks stay on 'their' tier too long. After 7-8 weeks, force them to move by shutting off the water alternately on each tier, for example for a couple of hours in the afternoon. Thirst will make them go in search of water themselves and they will learn to move between the different tiers. Make sure no hens become dehydrated if they really can't find water.

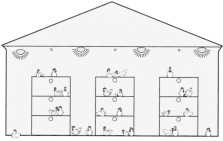

Daytime
- main lighting on
- rope lights off
- lure lights off

→ chickens in whole house

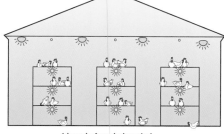

1 hour before dark period
- dim main lighting
- rope lights on
- lure lights off
→ chickens at the top stay there
→ chickens on the ground go to the bottom and middle tiers

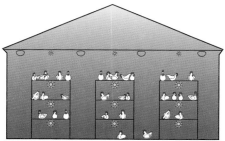

1/2 hour before dark period
- main lights off
- dim rope lighting
- lure lights on

→ last chickens go into the tiers

Dark
- main lights off
- rope lights off
- lure lights off

→ all chickens in system

Seeing the light

To enable efficient manure collection and to maintain good litter quality, you will want the chickens to sleep at the top in the system. Chickens are attracted to the light. Make use of this by operating the lights in the various compartments in the house separately. If you want them to be on perches or in the system in the evening, put the lights out in these places last. You could provide additional dimming lights at the top of the house, for example. If you want the chickens to be in the scratching area during the day, make the light brightest there.

Vaccinations

Reaction to vaccination: a good signal?

A reaction to a vaccination is a signal from the immune system that the vaccine has taken effect. After the first drinking water or spray vaccinations against Newcastle disease or IB, the chickens will be a little unwell for a few days. You can tell the quality of the vaccination from whether all the chickens show the same reaction to it (good sign) or whether it 'rolls' through the flock (vaccination initially only affects some birds). Stress and a poor house climate (dust and ammonia) can worsen a reaction to a vaccination. If the birds are feverish, make sure the house is properly ventilated. You might need to give them extra vitamins and minerals in the water.

Aviary rearing, vaccination misery?

Are the chicks still shut up in the system, has the poultry paper gone, and do they still need to be vaccinated against coccidiosis or Gumboro disease? Before these vaccinations take effect, it is important to recirculate via the manure or litter. Use thicker paper or opt for drinking water vaccinations instead of the spray version. Don't allow the chicks to eat before vaccinating them. If they are full and heavier, it is more difficult to get them into the system and they will become distressed more quickly if they sit on each other.

Spray and drinking water vaccinations

With spray and drinking water vaccinations, all birds must ingest sufficient live vaccine particles. You can make sure of this as follows:

- Don't allow the chicks/hens to drink before they are vaccinated, so that they are thirsty and soon empty the pipe containing the vaccine. Allowing the vaccine to stand for more than two hours will compromise the quality.
- Prepare enough vaccine solution.
- Use a stabiliser that not only protects the vaccination virus but also has a distinctive colour: peptone, skimmed milk or special dye.
- Check that the vaccine reaches the very back of the house by drawing some liquid there.

Signals of poorly performed vaccinations

This hen received a injection in the chest. The needle was inserted too low, touching the liver. This animal is in shock.

Here you can see what happens when you inject too low in the chest.

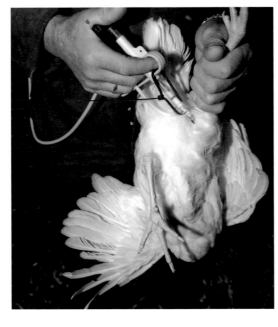

Minimise the stress of the combined vaccination at 12 weeks. Prevent suffocation by providing sufficient ventilation and preventing the birds from crawling all over each other. Treat the birds with respect and in an animal-friendly way.

The right way to vaccinate

A vaccination plan is a guideline for the administration of vaccinations. But in order to achieve the desired effect and avoid adverse side-effects, the vaccination needs to be administered properly.

Right

Wrong

Make sure the equipment (filters, o-rings) is clean on the inside and outside.

Right

Wrong

Use a filter to prevent any sediment and other impurities from getting into the spray and blocking the nozzle.

Right

Wrong

For hygiene reasons, but also for your own safety, always wear gloves. And open the flacon under water.

Right

Wrong

If possible, use a vaccine containing a dye so you can see whether all the birds have taken it.

From small to big in 18 weeks

Day-old chicks grow into sexually mature layers in just over four months. The development takes place on many different levels.

The last days in the hatchery

Before they hatch, the chicks communicate with each other to encourage each other to peck their way out of the shell. After breaking the shells the chicks are just about exhausted and rest while they dry off. All their reflexes are present straight away. Day-old chicks flap their wings as they drop off one moving conveyor onto the next in the hatchery. If they are lying on their backs, they turn over straight away. In the hatchery the chicks undergo several treatments such as sexing, spray vaccination against infectious bronchitis and an injected vaccination against Marek's disease.

Week 1-2

In the first few days they develop species-specific behaviour:
- they peck at everything to find out what is edible and to find something to drink;
- they eat their starter feed off poultry paper or feeding plates;
- they learn to scratch in the ground and take dust baths;
- play behaviour; running around together;
- they learn to roost during the day;
- the gastrointestinal system develops during the first week. Everything must be geared towards ensuring that this development is not interrupted.

Depending on the house, the poultry farmer will do the following
- aviary: chicks shut up on the middle tier;
- house with slats; chicks shut up on slats and/or in scratching area;
- beak trimming;
- vaccinations.

Week 5-6

Maximum physical development takes place in these weeks. All down has to be replaced by juvenile feathers (first moult). The skeleton is 50% complete.

Week 9-10

The birds are now almost fully grown in terms of size, but not in terms of muscle development and fat deposition. A partial moult takes place during this period. Body feathers are replaced but tail feathers remain (second moult). Provided the flock is sufficiently uniform and is above the normal weight (i.e. not on the basis of age), you can slow down the increase of feed supply. To prevent unnecessary nutrient intake, switch to a phase II grower feed that contains less protein. This approach will result in efficient birds in the laying period.

Week 3-4

Chicks learn to feed from feed troughs or pans. Switch from starter feed to grower feed (phase 1).

Tasks for the poultry farmer:
- if available, provide a scratching area.
- first vaccinations via drinking water.

Week 7-8

During these weeks, hens are eager to be fed: let them eat all the feed in the chain feeder once or twice a day to combat selection.
Sometimes there will also be a partial moult which makes the chicks more susceptible to problems. The chicks fight to establish a (temporary) pecking order. Time for vaccinations.

Moult during rearing

Rearing hens moult four times. One complete moult and three partial moults. The order in which feathers moult follows a specific pattern. The first row of feathers is most important for determining the moulting speed.

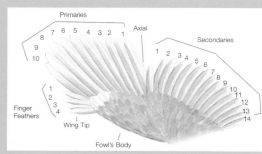

Order of moulting

First row:
1, 2, 3, 4, 5, 6, 7, 8, 9, 10

Second row:
11, 12, 13, 14, 10, 2, 3, 4, 5, 6, 7, 8, 9, 1, axial feather

Source: Ron Joerissen

Critical periods during development

Not all parts of the hen grow at the same pace; a different part grows stronger in each phase.
In critical periods of rapid growth, chickens are particularly vulnerable. If something goes wrong then, their development will be impaired, resulting in the chicken coming into lay later or not achieving maximum production.

During periods of slower growth (roughly weeks 10-15), the chicken is able to cope better, and restricting its feed can in fact be a good idea. For the layer farmer, the second critical period is particularly important as this is the time when the flock is set up: an extra reason to provide optimal care.

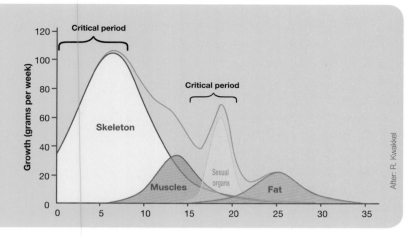

After: R. Kwakkel

Week 11-12
During these weeks, administer vaccinations in the form of eye drops, wing injections and breast injections.

Week 13-14
The second part of the partial moult starts in weeks 12-13. It continues until week 16. Interruptions in the moulting process can be seen straight away in the replacement of the wing feathers. Stress factors and vaccination plans affect the start and end of this moult. Oviducts and ovaries start to develop. Immunity continues to build up.

Week 17-18
The chicks are transferred to the laying farm.

Growth rate wing feathers

A feather grows 75% of its final length in the first three weeks. The last 25% also takes 3 weeks to develop! So a new feather is fully grown in 6 weeks time.

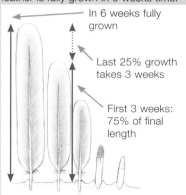

In 6 weeks fully grown

Last 25% growth takes 3 weeks

First 3 weeks: 75% of final length

Egged on from all sides

The changes a hen undergoes during her development are partly genetically pre-ordained: which organ grows and when, which behaviour is learned and when, and when the feathers are shed. Many external influences also affect her development. She is prepared for the production phase via the lighting programme and the composition of the feed. Other influences include the vaccination plan and beak trimming. In the long term these
treatments increase the hen's chances of survival, but in the short term she has to deal with stress, pain and reactions to vaccinations.
So every development stage has its own points for concern for the poultry farmer.

Week 15-16
A chick is at its most vulnerable in weeks 16-20. The skeleton is 95% complete. The laying organs begin to develop now. This means a rapid increase in body weight: this is caused by fluid retention rather than higher feed intake.
The sound changes: the hens begin to cluck. The hens get colour on their heads and the combs get bigger. The final vaccinations are administered. Do a final check of blood samples, weight and uniformity. Check the wing feathers to make sure the moult has proceeded properly, because this is an important signal as to whether the chick was raised properly.

Feather pecking during rearing

Feather pecking among rearing hens is greatly underestimated: more pecking goes on than is assumed, and if feather pecking does take place the impact in the laying period is greater than is thought. There are various signs of feather pecking at an early age:

- Feathers lying on the ground disappear (they are eaten).
- You can hear cries of pain every now and again (when a feather is pulled out).
- You can see injuries on the hens. Warning: Feather pecking among chicks is much more subtle than among adult chickens. You will rarely see bald patches on chicks.

Risks and prevention

- Boring environment. Chicks naturally peck the ground. If there is nothing of interest lying around (feed, litter), they will start pecking other things. Prevention: feed on feed plates or paper as long as possible and provide litter.

- Let the chicks out of the system or off the slats as early as possible.
- Moulting periods. During moulting periods, chickens have untidy plumage. This encourages them to pull out feathers. Prevention: provide a distraction or dim the lights.
- Lack of water and feed, feeding structure not right, selective eating, need for fibre. Poultry feed contains very little fibre, which is needed for good digestion. Chicks go in search of edible things that have texture. They start with wood shavings and feathers lying on the ground. Then they pull out each other's feathers. Prevention: give fibre in the feed, lucerne hay or extra litter.
- Redirected social behaviour. In large groups and high occupancy situations, chickens always encounter strangers whom they peck to get to know. Pecking can become habitual. Prevention: lower occupancy or smaller flocks.
- Poor house climate (carbon dioxide, ammonia, hot and dusty)
- High light intensity
- Beginning of laying
- Beware of a high occupancy. The chicks should have enough space
- Offer perches starting at the first week or other elevations, so that they can flee from each other.

If you put the chicks on wood shavings from day one, as in this photo, there is less chance of feather pecking.

Recognising pecking

If at the age of 16 weeks 20% of the birds are displaying symptoms of feather pecking....

... all the chickens in the flock will have bald backs by 35 weeks.

Beak trimming

Feather picking damage and cannibalism have until now been prevented with beak trimming. Beak trimming is currently allowed under the Dutch Animal Health and Welfare Act, but this comes to an end in 2011. Research is being carried out into possible alternatives.

Definitions and the law

Beak trimming is the removal of part of the beak. The wound is cauterised immediately with the heated blade. Under EU legislation, it must be done before the chick is 10 days old. At this early age the intervention is less painful for the chick and the risk of chronic pain is small, as long as no more than one third of the beak tip is removed. De-beaking, which is no longer permitted, took place at 6 weeks. Because the beak regrows, some non-European countries repeat the treatment at 10-14 weeks.

Advantages of beak trimming

+ Chickens with trimmed beaks are less able to feather pick. The damage caused by feather picking is less.
+ Better plumage means lower feed intake and lower feed conversion.
+ Losses through cannibalism are reduced.
+ Beak trimming improves the welfare of chickens which would otherwise be victims, leading to an economic benefit.

Disadvantages of beak trimming

− It is an intervention on the chicken; you should ideally create an environment in which this intervention is not needed.
− Trimming is painful, and some birds are left with chronic pain after de-beaking.
− Chickens with trimmed beaks can use their beaks less effectively for other things like eating and preening.
− Interventions on birds are bad for the public image of the sector.
− Beak trimming costs money.

Beak trimmed at 9 days. A good trimmer does not remove more than one third of the part between the nostril and the beak tip. This causes very little reaction from the chickens. Some flocks eat and drink slightly less.

Beak cut at 6 weeks. De-beaking retards growth by 10 days and there is a high risk of chronic pain. This is no longer permitted.

Example of incorrect trimming: only the top beak has been cut off. Badly de-beaked chickens waste more food.

Smooth transition

To ensure that as the rearer you are optimally committed and motivated to do your job, it is essential to know what the outcome of your work is. But in practice there is little or no contact between the rearer and the laying hen farmer. As the laying hen farmer, you may miss out on opportunities to ensure a smooth transition from rearing to laying. Make sure you discuss your requirements properly with the rearer. For example, go and visit the rearing farm towards at the beginning and at the end of the rearing period (taking all the necessary hygiene measures, of course). Then you can see how your birds are doing and make your wishes known: the amount of light, training the birds to use the whole house, and so on. Keep in regular touch with the rearers.

The nitty-gritties

It goes without saying that you will make arrangements about lots of aspects like vaccinations (in consultation with the vet), the age of transfer and light stimulation. But don't forget extras like gizzard grit, a higher fibre content in the feed, litter, scattered grain, raw feed and perches. Tell the rearer what you understand by a good hen.

Gizzard grit forms the chicken's teeth. It is not always given as standard in the rearing stage even though it can contribute to good digestion. Five grams at 5-6 weeks and again at 10-11 weeks is plenty.

What to ask the rearer

- Were there any health problems? What was the loss rate (rearing list)? Did you remove any birds, and why? How were they dealt with?
- Were any particular actions needed, e.g. later introduction of hens? If so, why?
- What are the feeding and lighting times?
- Check the vaccination card to see whether the vaccinations were correctly done and ask about any irregularities.
- Ask for the results of blood tests.

By assessing the hens together you can anticipate likely problems such as feather pecking at an early stage and adjust the rearing process if necessary.

Autopsy of a few pullets by the veterinary authorities provides information on the health status of the flock. For example intestinal health. Necessary treatment can then start at the rearing farm. At the end of the rearing period, medicines can still be used that are not permitted during laying.

Check to see that beaks have been properly trimmed, i.e. that the same amount has been removed from all birds. If it has not, as in the photograph, you may have problems with feed wastage. The hen will also be less able to look after her feathers.

Checklist for visiting the rearer

✔ Physical development. Look at the size of the comb, the colour on the head and in particular: the moulting stage (wing feathers, see pages 67 and 49). Are the comb size and colour uniform? Pick chickens up in different places in the house.

✔ Weight and uniformity. Are there a lot of small chicks? If so, ask why.

✔ Don't accept underweight specimens.

✔ Feather pecking. Are there signs of it?

✔ Light intensity. Ask the rearer to show you what light intensity he keeps the chickens in when there is no-one in the house. Golden rule: the light intensity should be at least the same as or lower than in the laying house.

✔ Climate. Is there condensation on the walls? How are the chickens spread out in the house? Can you smell ammonia?

✔ Health. Have the birds been given preventative treatment against worms? Are there red mites in the house?

LOOK-THINK-ACT

Down feathers on the floor?

When you visit the rearer, check whether there are down feathers in the litter. If there aren't, they have been eaten: a signal that the chicks are lacking in something, e.g. texture in the food. Ask the rearer to add lucerne hay or another high-fibre product to the feed.

CHAPTER 4

Laying hens

Laying percentage and egg weight depend on the breed of hen and the feed. The ideal weights for eggs for the table are sizes M (53-63 g) and L (63-73 g). XL is also fine provided the shells are of good quality. You can make the best returns from eggs if you take market demand into account.

Eggs are the main source of income on a laying hen farm. But all sorts of things are involved in achieving a high laying percentage and good quality eggs.

Schedules aren't written in stone

Don't apply schedules blindly. Look in particular at the development of the chickens. For example, give the chickens extra light if they have shed all their feathers. If they have been reared well, this will be at weeks 17 and 18, but this is not written in stone.

You want the hens to come into lay at the same time. So make sure that as many as possible have the same body weight and are in top condition when you put them in the laying house.

Keep in regular contact with the rearer. If there are a lot of hens at the same stage of development, you can manage them well with feeding and lighting pro-

grammes. So fewer hens will come into lay early or late. Flocks that come into lay early are often unstable and worn out before their time. They take in too little feed, their body weight is too low, the weight of the eggs is too low, the quality of the eggshells is poor, they have poor laying persistence, higher mortality and a greater risk of bad plumage.

> ### Tip
>
> An extra week of laying gives you more benefits than a week shorter rearing period. So don't let your chicks be delivered before 17-18 weeks of age. Remark: hens kept on floor systems should have sufficient time (1 week) to get used to their new environment, this is not an issue at cage-systems.

The ideal curves

Egg production is well under way at around 20 weeks, and the peak laying percentage is achieved at around 28 to 30 weeks. The egg weight should grow quickly to 60g at 30 weeks, after which it will gradually decrease by about 0.1g per week. Follow the laying percentage, feed and water intake and egg weight carefully, and intervene if production lags behind or starts to dip too soon.

A uniform flock of sufficient weight gives the best chance of eggs of the right weight at the start of the laying period and is also easier to manage. If you leave a flock in rearing for a week longer (18 instead of 17 weeks) they will have had more time to recover from the vaccinations and build up good resistance. They will therefore perform better under stress (transport from rearing to laying farm). You can also stimulate the hens with light slightly later, so the first eggs will be laid later and will therefore be heavier.

If the egg weight stays low, check the health of the flock and the feed quality. Also watch the weight development of the hens. During the first 10 production weeks, weigh the hens once a week at the same time of day. Automatic weighing is even better because it saves work and provides an accurate picture of the hens' weight during the entire cycle.

If disease is not a factor, adjust the feed. Discuss this with your feed supplier. For example, more methionine and linoleic acid can influence the weight of the egg. Make sure the eggs do not get too heavy (if so, reduce the methionine and linoleic acid). Because of the risk of feather pecking, don't restrict the feed.

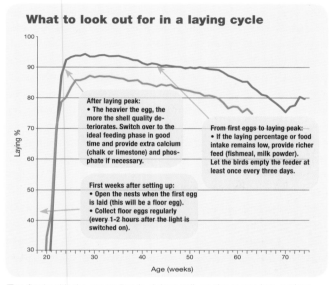

What to look out for in a laying cycle

After laying peak:
- The heavier the egg, the more the shell quality deteriorates. Switch over to the ideal feeding phase in good time and provide extra calcium (chalk or limestone) and phosphate if necessary.

From first eggs to laying peak:
- If the laying percentage or food intake remains low, provide richer feed (fishmeal, milk powder). Let the birds empty the feeder at least once every three days.

First weeks after setting up:
- Open the nests when the first egg is laid (this will be a floor egg).
- Collect floor eggs regularly (every 1-2 hours after the light is switched on).

The flock with the green line is doing well, as the curve has a clear peak above 90%. The flock with the red line is doing less well. A poor peak and a too low laying percentage for the whole period which could not be prevented. Up to week 22 everything seemed fine...

Moulting as a signal

What do you assess at the start of a new couple? Body weight, uniformity and age do not say everything about the development of the hens. The moulting stage of the hens also tells you a lot. The number of moulted wing feathers is a measure of the physical development of the hen. See also page 45.

Note the primaries from outside to inside. They have a flowing form in terms of length. This hen has moulted all its feathers. She is more than is sufficiently developed to be able to lay.

The two feathers on the far right are older and still have to be moulted. This hen is not sufficiently developed and is not yet laying any eggs. The difference between already moulted feathers (rounded) and not yet moulted feathers (pointed) is clearly visible.

Feed and feed management

You can use feed to control development, production and behaviour. The rearing and production periods consist of different phases, each with its own requirements for proportions of nutrients. The laying hen develops a skeleton and plumage from weeks 6 to 15. They also need to keep growing well during this time. Starting at 15 weeks of age, they develop the laying organs and a fat reserve.

Selective intake

Chickens prefer the coarse components of their feed. But the finer components also contain essential ingredients. Selective intake can be controlled by checking whether there are still enough coarse components in the feeder after 10 minutes. Different sized components must be evenly distributed to avoid selection. Tailor your feed management towards ensuring that all the chickens take in the same nutrients: the most dominant hens will make a bee-line for the coarse components.

When are the component sizes badly distributed?
1. Indication: What's left in the feeder after 10 minutes
2. Observe: Demixing in the silo
3. Talk to the feed supplier about this.

Once a hen is laying, the time of day is also important. Don't feed while the hens are laying, for example; keep things calm in the house. Make sure they go to roost at night with a full stomach.

To stimulate the feed intake of a poorly reared flock, add 1-2% fishmeal or adjust the feeding plan for a week.

Assessing the structure of the feed

The structure of the feed can be measured by visual observation. Sometimes the structure will look reasonable or good, but the chickens' feed intake will still be very selective. In the trough you can see the extent to which the chickens are feeding selectively.

Grower feed with a good structure. There is relatively little difference between coarse and fine components.

Even in the last bit of feed in the chain feeder, coarse components are visible. All animals took in the same nutrients

All coarse components have disappeared from the feed. The hens have evidently been looking for coarse components. And especially the dominant animals will have eaten the maize and wheat.

Feed and light

With feed and light you influence development, production and behaviour. In the rearing period good management transforms a small one-day-chick into a beautiful laying hen.

Phase 1: 0-6 weeks

The first three weeks the animals need to take in ample amounts of nutrients. From thee weeks on, they have to learn that they won't get feed the whole day. After feeding it means: when the feed is finished, it is finished! During this period the moulting from down to feathers be completed. Furthermore, this period is an important base for a good skeleton.

Phase 2: 7-15 weeks

In this period there are two occasions that animals partly moult. These are from week 7 to 9 and from week 12 to 16: always important phases in their development. Pay extra attention during these vulnerable periods.

Phase 3: 16-20 weeks

The hen has to get ready for laying. The animals have to grow well because of the development of the laying organs. At the same time there is again a partial moult from week 19 to 21. This is a very critical period in which much can go wrong because of which the animals don't become beautiful but poorly performing laying hens.

Phase 4: 21-30 weeks

During this period the animals start laying, but are not completely full grown. Ensure that the animals keep growing, but not by providing feed the whole day. They have to stay eager for feed and not waist feed. You accomplish this by making sure that the feeding system is completely empty at least once a day. Just like in the rearing period.

Lighting and feeding programmes

The lighting programme plays a major role in the development of the animal and the later laying performance. The basics are simple: a decreasing day length or continuous short day inhibits the natural sexual maturity and a increasing day length stimulates this (also see page 46).

Phase feeding for layers

Layers have a different need for energy and protein in each phase. Phase feeding enables you to control the egg weight better. You will also feed less protein over the whole cycle (less N and P), so you will save money. There is no such thing as a standard recommendation or plan for when to switch. When pullets arrive on the laying farm, you can opt to continue feeding rearing feed 2 for another week or start the follow-on feed - pre-lay feed or starter feed - straight away. The latter two are designed to increase the feed intake capacity so that the hens grow and their laying organs continue to develop: essential for laying percentage and egg mass. At 19-20 weeks you can switch to laying feed if the laying percentage is between 5 and 25.

Development visualised

Growth is not the same as development. Even when the skeleton is full grown, the hens continue to develop. And their needs are different during this phase of her development.

A slim hen at 10 weeks of age, with full plumage. This hen will not grow much more in terms of length. The skeleton is almost full grown. When you touch the skin at the breast of this hen, you will feel almost no fat.

A big hen at 46 weeks of age. Starting at 10 weeks, this hen has developed quite a musclular chest, with a thin layer of fat under the skin. The round belly shows the development of the laying organs.

Diluting the feed with raw feed

The more time chickens spend feeding and foraging for food (scratching, scraping the ground and pecking), the happier they are. In a non-cage system you can encourage this behaviour with raw feed (e.g. lucerne hay) or loose grains in the scratching area. In a cage system you can dilute the laying feed with ground raw feed. Chickens compensate for the diluted feed by eating more of it. Diluting down to 10-15% has no adverse effects on production. Supplementary feeding or diluting usually produces healthier chickens, lower mortality and less risk of feather pecking.

Scattering grain activates their natural behaviour and encourages the hens to spread well throughout the house.

Feeding in hot weather

Hens often eat less in hot weather. This mainly has implications for older rearing hens and hens aged up to about 35 weeks. An energy or protein deficiency will soon result in slower growth, lower egg production and higher mortality. A period of two hot weeks can cause financial losses of as much as 80 euro cents per free-range hen.

The shell quality is also poorer because of the extra excretion of minerals, higher blood pH and lower calcium intake. They also need more vitamin C than they can produce or absorb themselves. Modified feeds can help, as can adding vitamin C to the drinking water. Ask your feed supplier about the modified feeds available.

Deficiency signal: eating feathers

Are there down feathers in the litter? If the hens are eating the down, there is stress in the flock. This stress causes the gastrointestinal-system of the hen to malfunction. The animal wants to compensate this by eating parts with structure. These are, among others, feathers.

This stress can be caused by:

- house climate
- lack of structure in the feed
- shortage of nutrients
- infections.

Often it is a combination of these factors. Always involve your feed supplier and change the feed composition if necessary. For example, provide more high fibre products. Don't forget to consult the vet.

What to look out for in feeding systems

Make sure the feeder is long enough so that all the birds have a chance to feed. Taking account of the size of a laying hen, 15 centimetres of space per bird is needed at the feeder to allow them all to feed at the same time. This is slightly more than the legal requirement. If hens are reared in a different feeding system than the one used in the laying phase, make sure they are not too frightened by the new system.

Tip

Take a sample of feed from every delivery. If something goes wrong later, you can always check whether it has anything to do with the feed. Store up to about ten samples.

Length of the trough

With the current legal requirements all animals will never be able to eat at the same time. Take this fact into consideration in your daily routines. Preventing selective intake will ensure that also the more submissive hens get what they need.

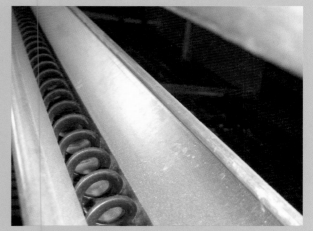

Trough with chain feeder

A chain transports feed from a storage bin and distributes it along the feeder trough. The speed varies between 4 and 20 m per minute. With a faster chain there is less risk of selective feeding and less spillage. A grill above the feeder troughs prevents pullets from crawling into the troughs and contaminating the feed with droppings. Also check the height of the feed. If the layer is thicker, the chain will not get in the way and the birds can select feed more easily.

Trough with spiral

The spiral distributes the feed over the trough and stops the hens throwing it to the side, so they spill less.

Feeding pans

Feeding pans are height adjustable. Make sure the feed is evenly distributed over all pans. Spillage can be a problem, but it depends to a large degree on how the system is installed. The pans must be hung at the right height and it is important to feed 'in blocks', meaning that in a short time all pans are filled.

Water

On average, laying hens take in 1.6 to 2 times more water than feed. They drink regularly and in small amounts. The volume of daily water intake is a good indicator of the health of the flock.

If the birds start to drink more, first look at the ambient temperature and the salt content of the feed as a potential cause. Then assess the health status and consult a vet if necessary. The drinking water should taste pleasant and must not contain any hazardous substances or impurities. Impurities can pose a risk to food safety via the meat or eggs.

Water also serves as a solvent for medicines and vaccines. This requires clean water and properly functioning pipes.

Therefore, rinse the pipes in advance. And also rinse them after administering medicines to prevent residues.

If the hens are drinking too little, first check that the water system is working properly. The water pressure must not be too low. You also don't want the water pressure in the drinking line to be too high as this can cause spillage and lower water intake as the hens have to push harder on the nipple. Check the water quality when the system is working properly and the nipple is at the right height.

The drinking water must be readily available. The standard for hens in floor systems is 1 drinker nipple or cup per 10 birds or 1 cm per bird (round drinkers). In traditional battery cages, 2 drinker nipples or cups must be available. These days, drinker nipples are of such good quality that drip trays are no longer necessary. Drip trays are susceptible to fouling.

Check the water:

1. generally on the meter (automatically)
2. per nipple line: the level at the air vent (daily).
3. per nipple (at least once every two months)

Water quality

Water can contain dangerous, undesirable substances that will end up inside the chicken. The quality of mains water is generally good. But this may not be the case with the water from your own source. In order to keep your water quality up to standard, technical aids such as a deionisation system or a reverse osmosis system (which filters all substances out of the water) can be used. Also clean water pipes well and avoid sagging to prevent fungal growth. If you suspect the drinking water might be contaminated, have it tested.

Cause	Dangerous (mg/l)	Signal
Nitrite	> 1,0	Lower oxygen uptake in the blood, result: comb, lobes and head turn blue, animal becomes lethargic. Reduced fertility
Nitrate (can be converted into nitrite)	> 200	Respiratory infections
Sodium	> 200 [1]	Diarrhoea Cerebral symptoms: wryneck and lameness
Chloride	> 300 [1]	Reduced feed intake
Sulphide, conversion from sulphate under the influence of certain bacteria	> 250	Blocked nerve conduction; smell of rotten eggs
Iron	> 5,0	Intestinal dysfunction
E. coli	> 100 (kve/ml)	Intestinal dysfunction
Mycotoxins (produced by moulds)	No threshold	Weaker resistance

[1]: for laying hens > 600 mg/l chloride and > 400 mg/l sodium

Testing the waters

You can get a quick initial impression of the water quality by pouring some water into a transparent bottle and examining the colour, clarity, sediment and smell. Take the water from the drinking places at the back of the house. It's easy to assess; every parameter is rated good, moderate or poor.

Colour: good (absolutely colourless); moderate (slight discolouration); poor (distinct colour; yellow, brown etc.).
Clarity: good (completely clear); moderate (cloudy but still transparent); poor (opaque).
Sediment: good (water free from particles); moderate (a few particles); poor (bottom is entirely covered with mud or iron particles).
Smell: good (absolutely odourless); moderate (slight smell); poor (strong smell of rotten eggs).

- All parts good: 15% chance that the water is unsuitable.
- All parts poor: the water is always unsuitable.
- Some parts moderate: 35-75% chance that the water is unsuitable.

Test the water at least twice a year. Sample it at the end of the nipple line or the end of the system. Ask yourself: would I drink this water myself? If not, why would your chickens.

colour: good, clarity: good

colour: poor, clarity: good

colour: poor, clarity: poor

colour and clarity good; sediment poor

Pros and cons of drinking water systems

Drinking water system	Advantages	Disadvantage
Round drinkers	+ Water readily available + Water level and suspension height easy to regulate	− Open system, not always fresh, more chance of contamination − Contributes to higher relative humidity in the house − Spillage
Drinking nipples	+ Closed system, water always fresh + Very little spillage + Lots of room to walk around	− High investment costs − Water dispensing harder to control
Drinking cups	+ Water readily available + Easy to check for blockages	− High investment costs − More chance of contamination − Less room to walk around

External egg quality

External quality criteria of consumer eggs are weight, colour, shape, strength and cleanliness of the shell. You can tell a good deal from the outside of an egg. Defects, damage or dirty shells are directly related to the health status of the hens, the composition of the feed and/or parts of the housing.

Dirty shells are caused by blood, manure, dust, wet litter, egg pulp, red mites, mould or fly droppings.

Dust stripes on the eggs

Dust rings are caused by eggs rolling on dirty floors. In cages, dust on the grid can cause dust rings. Take a close look at the route of the egg in the house and check that there is no dust and dirt accumulating along it. Also make sure that the shells are dry before they roll on to the conveyor. You can do this with an egg saver. The egg saver not only ensures that the egg lands on the belt in one piece but also dry, so it is less likely to collect dirt and dust. Of course, the eggs should not remain in the nests too long. Clean the egg conveyors regularly. The presence of small blood specks on the shell indicates a severe red mite infestation. These are red mites that were squashed when the egg rolled over the egg conveyor.

Blood on the shell

Blood on the shell comes from a damaged vent caused by too heavy eggs or vent pecking.

Manure on the shell

Manure on the shell could be the result of intestinal diseases which cause the hens to produce thin manure. Thin manure can also be caused by incorrect feed composition. Contact your feed supplier or vet. Also check the nest expulsion system. If it is not working properly or it closes too late, eggs can be soiled by dirty nest floors. Hen-pecked hens may hide in the nests and defecate there, soiling the eggs. In addition, wet litter can result in dirty feet which can soil the eggs. Finally, try spreading out feeds so that most of the manure is not produced when the eggs are being laid. Also check the ventilation. Incorrect underpressure can make the litter space too damp.

Damage after laying

Eggs can get damaged and show breaks, hairline cracks, dents or holes after laying. Carefully check the route the egg follows: are the eggs rolling too hard, are they rolling against each other anywhere, are the transitions between conveyors properly aligned? The more eggs there are on the collection belt, the more breakages and cracks you can expect. So make sure you collect often enough: at least twice per day. Every system has points to watch out for. If 95% of eggs in a colony house arrive in the same place on the egg conveyor, there will be a greater chance of damage. Pull the egg conveyor along a couple of times to spread out the eggs.

Check whether there are any specific problem places using an electronic egg (a transparent egg with built-in electronics) or by collecting eggs in certain places and candling them.

Heavier eggs laid at the end of the laying period can have weaker shells. Adjust the calcium content of the feed in good time and provide extra calcium. Make sure the hens feed well before the dark period starts, as shells are mainly formed at night. There may also be a problem with the hens' feed intake (disease, high temperatures).

An egg with a crack or break on the side. The shell was damaged when the egg rolled off. A crack or break at the blunt end indicates that the nest floor is too hard; the egg is damaged by falling on the floor when it is laid.

An electronic egg emits a light signal when it is jolted. This shows you where eggs can get damaged on a conveyor and in the packaging machine.

Shell defects that appear before laying

Pimples; local roughness, usually at the blunt end of the egg. This can be caused by infectious bronchitis.

The shell of this egg is ridged. The inside of the egg membrane was not completely filled with moisture and albumen when the shell calcified. Possible cause: infectious bronchitis.

A soft shelled egg missing part of its shell. Possible causes: Egg Drop Syndrome, Avian Influenza or rapid successive ovulations at the start of the laying period so the egg is laid before it is ready.

The egg tip is rougher and thinner and shows a clear separation from the healthy part of the shell: glassy tips. Cause: damaged laying organs. This can be caused by a specific Mycoplasma synoviae-strain.

Internal egg quality

Eggs go straight to consumers from the laying farm without any processing. So the egg quality must be good and the eggs must not contain any impurities. The internal aspects that determine the quality of an egg are flavour, residues, germs, inclusions and freshness.

Undesirable substances

Eggs must not contain any undesirable substances such as residues of antibiotics, antiparasitics, pesticides and environmental pollutants.

Destroy any eggs produced during the withdrawal period after administering medication. Consumers expect this level of care and honesty, and residues can cause health problems.

You can achieve a higher hygiene status with plastic trays than with pulp trays. Egg processing can for the most part be automated: pulp trays are less suitable for this. In addition, plastic pallets are becoming more and more widespread. Plastic trays are more hygienic, provided they are properly cleaned.

Flesh and blood specks

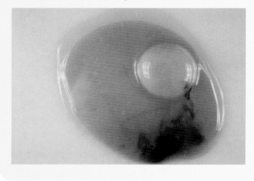

Flesh and blood specks are only visible when the eggs are candled at the packing station. Flesh specks are particles released from the oviduct. Blood specks are the result of the yolk sac being torn at a site with blood vessels. This can be caused by fright reactions or IB infections. Yolk sacs usually tear at sites with no blood vessels.

LOOK-THINK-ACT

What does a different yolk colour tell you?

The colour of the yolk is mainly influenced by the feed composition and the amount of colouring agent in the feed. If the yolk colour remains too pale, check the following:
- Was the feed intake lower, maybe because the weather was hot? If chickens eat less food, they will also consume less colouring agent.
- Was the hens' digestion poor due to an infection, for example? This would make the chickens less able to absorb the colouring agent in the feed.
- If you think the chickens were not sick or were eating normally, ask your feed supplier to adjust the feed.

Quality report from the egg wholesaler

As a poultry farmer, you not only have to respond to the signals from the chickens but also to those from your customer: the egg wholesaler. The wholesaler will check your eggs for various criteria. The quality report can tell you where improvements need to be made, such as egg weight, yolk colour and damage. If you keep an ongoing record, you can anticipate developments instead of only taking action when you get an alert from your packing centre.

Report parameters	Signal	Possible action, now or next flock
Average weight	Too light, too heavy	Amount and type of layer feed Choice of breed, hen weight from rearing farm
Yolk colour	Too light, too dark	Amount of red and yellow colouring agents in the feed, feed intake, intestinal and general health
Breaking strength	Weak shell	Layer feed, technical guidance, choice of breed
Haugh Units (HU; freshness)	Too low	Amount of protein in the feed, protection against IB, general health of the hen
Shell colour (brown eggs only)	Too light	Choice of breed in the next cycle
Staining	Dirt on eggs (including manure, dust, mites, fly droppings)	Good, modern laying nest, good layer feed, good bird health. Speed of the egg conveyor
Cracks (star cracks, shell membrane intact)	Too many cracked eggs	Egg collection system at the poultry farm (lift or packer), breaking strength too low
Hairline cracks (invisible to the naked eye, eggs burst open when cooked)	Too many hairline cracks	Egg collection system at the poultry farm (lift or packer), breaking strength too low
Open break	Too many open breaks	Egg pecking by hens, rough handling of eggs, breaking strength too low
Egg stamp	No stamp, incorrect code, not clearly legible	Adjust and maintain egg stamping machine

Fresh or old egg?

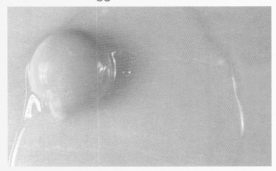 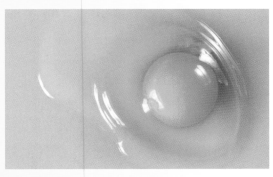

Old egg   *Fresh egg*

Temperature and moisture play a major role in egg storage. Eggs are usually picked up twice a week. In this case, the best storage temperature is 18°C. If they are stored for more than 10 days, 10-12°C is better. Avoid large temperature fluctuations to prevent condensation.
Condensation promotes the development of microorganisms on the shell (fungal growth) which can penetrate the pores and contaminate the contents. The relative humidity during storage influences moisture loss in the egg (resulting in weight and quality loss). Keep the humidity between 75 and 80%.
Poor storage conditions accelerate ageing of the egg.

What makes a nest attractive?

Correct position. Site the nests in a quiet spot if possible. Don't walk in front of the nests, don't inspect the nests during the morning laying peaks, and don't turn the egg belts off. Keep disruption to a minimum by not feeding during laying. Suspend a drinking water line in front of the laying nests and open these lines first in the mornings. That's how the chickens start their day at the nests.

Attractive nest floor: artificial grass or rubber studs. A good compromise between the preference of hen (chopped straw) and farmer (hygienic and efficient nests) is a nest floor of artificial grass or rubber studs. The chicken can scrape in it a bit, it's not dusty, it doesn't obstruct the egg collecting system and it's easy to clean.

Good light intensity. It should be lighter outside the nest than inside. This does not mean that the nest should be pitch dark. The hens still need to be able to see in the nest, otherwise they would be too frightened to go into it. Consider installing a dim light in any very dark nests. One lux should be sufficient.

Enough laying nests. You can never have too many nests. Communal nests are used almost exclusively these days. Nest space becomes restrictive more quickly for small groups of birds. About 125 cm^2 of nest space per hen is recommended in this case. For larger groups, the recommended space is 100 cm^2 per hen, while the statutory minimum is 83.3 cm^2 per hen (120 hens per square metre of nest).

Make the laying nests as attractive as possible for the hens so that they actually lay their eggs in them.

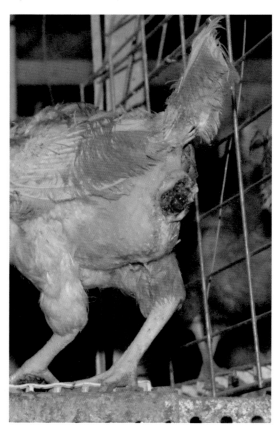

Bare and pecked vents can be a signal of too much light in the laying nests. The vent bulges during laying. If the nest is too light, hens notice this, which encourages them to pick at it.

Avoid floor eggs

Floor eggs will always end up on the egg belt in colony systems. The problem of floor eggs is greatest in floor and aviary systems. This costs money: you can't sell them as grade A, and some are lost by being trampled on or pecked. This makes your production seem lower than it actually is. It is important to remember this when you look for the cause of disappointing results. Rule of thumb: for every floor egg found, one is lost.

As soon as all the birds come into lay, you need to do all you can to prevent floor eggs. It is not just a question of the time the laying nests are opened; you also need to remove floor eggs often and, in particular, promptly. Prevention is better than cure.

An electric wire can solve the problem of floor eggs in corners. Don't use this preventatively because it increases the stress on the birds.

Risk factors for floor eggs

Not learning to jump properly during rearing
If the hens have not learned to overcome height differences in the rearing stage, they are less likely to move vertically to where the laying nests are located in the aviary system on the laying farm. This dramatically increases the risk of floor eggs. So make sure the house systems in the rearing and laying phases are as similar to each other as possible.

Shadowy places
If there are dark areas or shadowy places, increase the light intensity or fit supplementary lighting in places the main lighting doesn't reach. It can be useful to introduce a dim phase at the beginning of the day time period as well. Some laying hens often need to lay their eggs before the light goes on. These eggs will then land on the slats. A semi-dark period gives these early birds the opportunity to find nests while the rest are still asleep.

Attractive litter
A layer of litter is good for the hen, but also inviting to lay in. Prevent laying in the litter by providing sufficient light and collecting any eggs as soon as possible. This will stop other birds from laying eggs there. You will also disturb any chickens that want to lay there. Also disturb them while laying. This means: make several inspections of a starting flock early in the morning.

Laying nests difficult to access
It's difficult for the birds to get past each other when looking for a laying nest. Resting hens can block the nest entrance. Fit several perches or a grating in front of the nests. The hens can walk over them and get past each other to see which nests are occupied.

Draughty nests.
You can feel whether the nest is draughty by holding a wet hand in the nest. If the space under the nests is cold, there could be a draught in the nests caused by underpressure. This will discourage the hens from laying there. Solve this by putting an airtight panel under the nests. Draughts in the nests can also be caused by the incoming airflow.

Rearing birds without levels leads to problems if there is an aviary house on the laying farm.

It's dark under the rack, so there is a risk of floor eggs there.

Laying nests must be designed so that hens can get past each other when they are looking for somewhere to lay.

Gear management towards nesting peak

Hens are laying for ever longer periods: sometimes up to more than 100 days in succession. The first egg in a period is laid early in the morning. With present-day breeds the laying time hardly ever changes, while with earlier crosses the laying time would change and the hens sometimes missed a day. Most eggs are therefore laid in the morning. Gear your management towards this morning laying peak. A hen needs to be able to lay her eggs in peace. Give the birds light, feed and water more or less simultaneously in the morning. Then don't feed them for five to six hours, until most of the eggs have been laid. Run the chain feeder late in the evening so that there is still some feed in it in the morning. In the morning, don't run it until after the laying peak. This prevents the birds being lured out of the nests, causing disruption and more floor eggs.

Fear costs eggs

Make sure the hens get used to people. Fear of people will affect egg production and egg quality. Genuine panic reactions can even lead to higher bird losses and a higher risk of feather pecking due to the stress. It also makes it more difficult to perform health checks and catch hens. Put a radio on in the house, ideally with a programme that alternates music and speech. This will get the hens used to human sounds so they will take fright less easily.
Tips for getting chickens used to people:

Pop in to the hens several times a day, not always at the same time. Wearing different colour overalls helps as well.

Regularly scatter small amounts of grain by hand. The hens will associate the 'care giver' with a positive experience.

The more intriguing and richer the surroundings, the less anxious the hens will be in general. You could consider building a winter garden with perches and a raw feed dispenser.

LOOK-THINK-ACT

What does this mean?

This is an anxious flock. All the birds are trying to get away and they are piling up on top of each other. This could result in trampling and suffocation. Frightened hens in cages can't run away but they could injure themselves seriously. If hens are easily frightened, try and get them more accustomed to people by walking round or through them more often.

A second laying period?

Hens are laying for longer these days, so there is little reason to induce a second laying period. In emergencies or unforeseen circumstances, it is sometimes decided to force a moult. The moult lasts for four to six weeks, after which the second laying period lasts for six to eight months. The hens are made to moult by shortening the day length to a maximum of eight hours, providing low-energy feed such as wheat bran or oats, and after three to four weeks reverting the day length and feed to the original situation. Forcing a moult is precision work. Consult your advisor and abide by the statutory requirements; i.e. you must not withhold any feed or water from your birds. Interrupt the moulting process if necessary if the hens continue to lay. Continuing the process or further restricting the day length is bad for the health and welfare of your birds. Give extra grit to prevent the birds from becoming deficient in calcium and suffering skeletal defects.

Pecking, feather pecking and cannibalism?

When a poultry farmer talks about pecking, he refers to blood visible at the tailbase. It mainly happens to young birds that have just acquired their plumage. It is therefore important to act quickly. Remove the bird and spray it with something with an unpleasant taste and smell to stop other birds pecking at it. If you don't intervene fast and effectively, it will become a major problem which will ultimately get out of control. Feather pecking among rearing hens is underestimated and signals are misleading: the damage can be so subtle that you may not pick up on it at all, let alone take action. On adult hens you could see bald patches, but in rearing hens you often only notice a few covert feathers missing at the bottom of the back. You can recognise this by the protruding down feathers or bushy tail feathers. It is more noticeable on brown hens than white ones as the coverts are brown and the underfeathers are white. Genuine bald patches are very rare in the rearing phase. Because the symptoms are so subtle, the poultry farmer will often rate his flock as having a good plumage and no pecking. But if a few underfeathers are visible on 20% of the chickens at 16 weeks, most of the flock will have significant bald patches by 30 weeks.

Disadvantages and advantages of moulting

- The hens get out of rhythm which can lead to stress and abnormal behaviour (e.g. feather pecking and cannibalism).
  - Different moulting rates can affect the uniformity of the flock.
    - The proportion of oversized eggs can increase significantly.
      - Some vaccinations have to be repeated

+ Laying percentage of 85% at 2nd lay with a good flock.
  + Medicines can be administered during moult (no residues in egg, pay attention to waiting period.
    + By moulting, hens have a longer productive life, so rearing costs are lower.

Feather pecking and cannibalism are undesirable behaviour and occur in all husbandry systems.

Types of pecking

Scientists distinguish between two types of pecking: 'aggressive pecking' and 'feather pecking/cannibalism'. The signals from the chicken differ for each type. To be able to respond appropriately, you need to be able to recognise the signals. Feather pecking is often incorrectly described as aggressive behaviour. But aggressive pecking is normal behaviour, and feather pecking is abnormal behaviour which only occurs in captivity.

Aggressive pecking	Feather pecking
Aimed at the head	Not only to the head, but also the neck, breast, wings, side, back, tail or under the tail.
Aimed at a bird that gets under the feet of a higher ranking bird.	Aimed at birds that are standing quietly and eating or taking a dust bath.
A feather is sometimes pulled out, but it is never eaten.	Feathers that have been pulled out are frequently eaten.
It is only a sign of compromised welfare if it happens a great deal.	This behaviour always indicates a problem.

Difficult to reverse

Feather pecking and cannibalism are signs of reduced bird welfare and can be very costly. Feather pecking leads to higher feed intake and cannibalism leads to losses. Once feather pecking and cannibalism happen in a flock, they are very difficult to eradicate. So prevention is key.

Feather pecking is when a chicken pulls out and eats another chicken's feathers. Feather pecking is first visible at the bottom of the back, at the base of the tail. A bare chicken is more susceptible to injury and infections. Feather pecking has nothing to do with aggressive behaviour.

Cannibalism is when one bird eats the skin, tissue or organs of other birds, dead or alive. The area around the vent and the abdominal organs are the parts most prone to pecking.

Caged vs uncaged chickens

Feather pecking occurs in all husbandry systems. It is a bigger problem with uncaged chickens than with caged birds. Uncaged feather peckers in a large group can create more victims. It is also easier to keep chickens in a lower light level in a cage house. Lower light intensity means that the chickens are less active, which reduces feather pecking. It is not the case that there is no reason for feather pecking in caged birds.

Bare chickens cost money

Relationship between plumage and feed intake

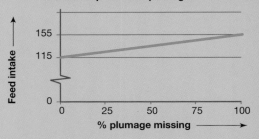

Feather pecking is bad for bird welfare and costs the poultry farmer money. A bare chicken eats 20% more food just to keep warm. Another rule of thumb: a chicken needs to eat 4 grams more per day for every 10% of feathers it loses. Bare chickens that move about a lot or go outdoors need even more feed.

Light and feather pecking

Dimming the light reduces feather pecking and cannibalism. Light therefore seems to be the cause of feather pecking and cannibalism. Darkening the house makes the birds less active.

How **red light** helps control cannibalism is not exactly clear. The idea behind red light is that contrasts on the plumage disappear so there are fewer targets to peck at. Red light also often reduces the light intensity and makes the chickens less active. However, red light and steady light intensity can also cause the birds to become more aggressive.

Feather pecking

The first sign of feather pecking is the disappearance of the feathers that are usually lying around on the ground. A little later you will hear the occasional screech: a victim screeching with pain when a feather is pulled out. After that, the hens will start to suffer injury. First very subtly: bald patches only occur later. By this time, the process can't be stopped.

Meat and bone meal in the feed

We don't yet know and understand everything. For example, why chickens start feather pecking later if they are fed meat and bone meal in their feed. Meat and bone meal has a different amino acid profile from vegetable proteins. The concentrations of some amino acids in the feed, although considered non-essential, are therefore much lower. Tests reveal that with meat and bone meal in the feed, feather pecking still happens but only at an older age than with feed containing vegetable protein.

Offer something new for the birds to peck on a regular basis, otherwise it will not help. Putting a few empty jerry cans in the house to peck on once will get you nowhere.

Causes of feather pecking

- incorrectly targeted pecking behaviour caused by a lack of litter (in the rearing phase)
- deficiency of fibre, minerals, vitamins or amino acids in the ration
- chronic gastroenteritis
- irritation by red mites;
- bad house climate
- boredom
- stress
- direct bright sunlight
- too high light intensity combined with one of the above factors.

Signals of feather pecking

Because of the difference in colour between coverts and underfeathers, feather pecking is more noticeable in brown chickens.

Chickens lose feathers every day, which normally remain on the ground. If feathers start disappearing from the ground, they are being eaten: a sure sign that there is something amiss in the flock.

Preventing feather pecking

Avoid all forms of stress in the broadest sense of the word. Here are a few examples:

- Choose a hen that is suitable for floor, aviary or free-range systems.
- Prevent floor eggs.
- Ensure a smooth transition from the rearing house to the laying house. You should not suddenly give chickens accustomed to a dark house a lot of light. Keep to the same times for switching the light on and off, feeding routines etc. Do not shut up the birds on the slats or in the system. If you do, understand that there will be very high occupancy and provide litter on the slats.
- Combat mites.
- Keep the chickens busy with dry, loose litter. Scatter grain or raw feed regularly to keep the place attractive.
- Provide distractions in the form of scattered grain, suspended ropes, aerated concrete blocks, peck blocks, corn cobs, grass etc. Chickens get tired of these 'toys' so regularly give them something new.

- Give the feed in meal form instead of granules.
- Thin the feed with high-fibre raw materials or give roughage such as silage maize, silage feed or lucerne hay. High-fibre products include ground oat hulls, lucerne meal, grass meal, ground straw, ground wood chips or sunflower seed flakes.

What to do about feather pecking

It is always difficult to track down the specific cause of feather pecking. There are often several things involved.

- Check the nutrient levels in the feed. Give extra vitamins and minerals to eliminate deficiencies.
- Dim the light or use a red light.
- Preventive measures can also help solve the problem, so provide distraction, treat the birds for red mites and worms and keep them as busy as possible with feeding measures and things to peck.

For these 11 week old hens, these aerated concreted blocks are a much loved pecking object.

This house has a scattering system suspended above the scratching area. Grain is scattered four times per day, about one-third of the daily ration. The core feed is matched to the scattering grain.

Cannibalism

Causes

- When an egg is laid, part of the intestine or oviduct emerges with it and stays there.
- Chickens that lay floor eggs literally expose their vents.
- Too much light in the nests. The vent always bulges out a little during laying, forming a target for cannibalism.
- Deficiency in the feed (protein, vitamins or minerals).
- Switching to less tasty feed.
- Injuries from sharp parts of the cages or house inventory are a target.
- Different chickens in the flock.
- Chickens that are too light weight are the first victims.

Action required

- Take action to prevent floor eggs.
- Don't light the nests or cover the opening.
- Every day, remove any weak, frightened, injured and dead chickens from the flock or place them in the sickbay.
- Aim for good uniformity (no poorly developed birds).
- Make sure that the eggs are not too heavy; this causes bloody vents.
- Check whether the outbreak has anything to do with a new feed supply or composition. Feed extra vitamins, minerals and salt.
- Dim the light or use a red light.
- Provide things to peck at, like aerated concrete blocks and roughage.
- If the cannibalism is feed-related, tell the feed supplier and get them to deliver new feed if necessary.

Dead chickens are very interesting to the other birds in the flock. Remove them immediately, as this can encourage cannibalism.

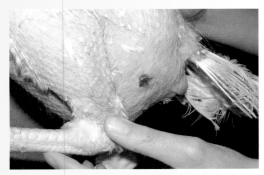

You can recognise cannibalism on dead birds because they will have been scavenged from behind. On living birds with bare patches you will see peck wounds, especially around the vent and on the laying stomach. This starts off small but can lead to terrible injuries.

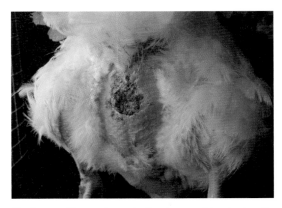

Feather pecking and cannibalism have nothing to do with aggression.

CHAPTER 5

Broilers

Broilers are bred for fast growth and development of plenty of breast meat. After seven days a good chick will weigh four times its initial weight. Its start in life plays a major role in how the cycle develops. Every breed has its own guidelines with regard to behaviour and care needs.

Their behaviour, water and feed intake and loss rates are indications of how the chicks are doing.

When the chicks come out of the delivery box, some of the chicks are already 48 hours old. Handling them in the hatchery, transporting them and placing them in the house causes stress. Four hours after they are set up in the house, the temperature of the litter should be between 35 and 37°C and the chicks will want to start feeding and drinking. Within 12 hours of setting them up, provide the chicks with a dark period of four hours to calm them down.

In the patio system, the hatching eggs are placed in the broiler chick house three days before the eggs hatch. The advantage of this is that the chicks do not have to be transported after hatching and can start feeding straight away.

Checking the chicks on arrival

Body temperature

On arrival, feel whether the chicks are hot or cold. Feel the feet and skin against your lips: this is the best way to feel the temperature. Repeat this when the chickens have been in the house for a couple of hours. If they are still cold, increase the temperature by a few degrees.

Comfort signals in day-old chicks

After being released, the chicks have to get used to their new environment before they go exploring. So it is normal for them to sit still for a while to begin with, but after about four hours they should start spreading out, exploring and feeding. If they do not, the litter or the air in the house is too cold. Cold will get them off to a bad start.

If they are sitting too close together on the first day, they will keep doing that if you don't react. This sows the seeds for poorly developed birds, resulting in uneven flock uniformity. If they stay sitting close together, they will also overheat. Try to spread out the chicks as soon as possible after their arrival by increasing the temperature and dimming the light slightly.

If young chicks all press up against the wall, it is too light. If the chicks are too cold, they will cheep loudly.

See also chapter 3 for information on assessing day-old chicks.

Differences between roosters and hens

Young roosters and young hens differ in weight. So when you weigh them manually you will know what you are holding. With older chicks, you can tell by the comb what sex they are. The rooster's comb has big teeth and is slightly rounded. The teeth on the hen's comb are more saw-like and the comb is upright. Rooster chicks also develop their feathers slightly less quickly and have a short tail.

Rooster (left) and hen (right)

Tip

- Get the chicks to spread out more in the house by walking from front to back and tapping on the wall. The chicks will be attracted by the sound and will disperse better.

Spreading out in the first hours

Four to six hours after being released, the chicks will start to spread out.

The chicks in this house have spread out well in the 24 hours since they were released.

Ventilation

How much you ventilate will not only depend on the temperature but also the humidity in the house, the speed of the air flow round the animals and the carbon dioxide level. If the carbon dioxide level is too high, the chicks will become lethargic. If you get a headache after working just above the height of the chicks for five minutes, the carbon dioxide level is 3500 ppm or higher, which means that ventilation is poor.

High humidity: higher wind chill factor

The skin temperature (wind chill factor) is related to the relative humidity. How high the relative humidity can be depends on the temperature. The norm for skin temperature is 90 + age of the chicks in weeks. The optimum level is RH + temperature.
An example: the chicks are 21 days old, the RH is 73% and the temperature is 24°C. The norm is 90 + 3 = 93. The level is 73 + 24 = 97. Conclusion: the air is too moist, so you should ventilate more.

These chicks are lying stretched out with their beaks open and you can see their throats going up and down. They are too hot.

Young chicks

Young chicks need warmth; they can only regulate their body temperature themselves after 3 to 4 days. Small one day old chicks, usually from young mother birds, will need a house that is 1-2° warmer than heavier chicks from older mother birds. If your hatchery does not tell you the age of the parent birds up front, ask them. Weigh your chicks on arrival so that you know what you are getting. Chicks weighing about 37-38 g will need more warmth than chicks weighing more than 42 g.

Older chicks

Older chicks produce heat themselves. If they can't expel the heat, they will grow less. In extreme cases, the bird will overheat and die (heat stress). Older chicks have a good feather covering except on the breast (their roosting place). Because they spend a lot of time lying down, this makes them particularly sensitive to the litter temperature. Too low a temperature will also inhibit growth because the chicks will not be active, and this will cause problems with litter quality.

These chicks are all the same age: there can be big differences in size even within one flock. These birds also need different amounts of warmth.

LOOK-THINK-ACT

House floor wet or dry?

What do you notice about the colour of the house floor? It's dark, so it's wet. That's because the house is too damp. In this case you should ventilate more. Check whether this is happening all over the house or only in certain places.

Distribution of the chicks in the house

Even distribution of the chicks throughout the house will promote growth (uniformity) and reduce mortality rates. Poor distribution will result in areas with poor litter, footpad problems and irritated breast skin. With bare, wet arms or wearing shorts, go and stand in the parts of the house where there are too few chicks and feel whether there is a draught there. Feel whether the litter feels cold. See whether there is a pattern and whether it has anything to do with the position of the lamps, fans, air intake etc. If you change the settings, give the chicks a couple of hours to adjust. Don't conclude too quickly that the change has not worked or is no good. Make a note of what you have changed.

Poor distribution among young chicks

The chicks are sitting close together.
The chicks are sitting close together and are not moving much. Feel the chicks and their feet to see whether they are cold.

The chicks are lying by the wall
More chicks are lying by the walls than in the middle of the house. They probably find it too light to rest and sleep. Dim the lights. They might also be too warm..

Good ventilation for older chicks

Poor ventilation for older chicks

If you cannot feel it yourself, do a smoke test to see how quickly the air is flowing through the house. You don't have to take the chicks out of the house to do this. There are several options:

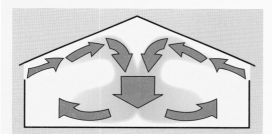

- The fresh, cold air in the middle sinks and there is little air movement at the sides.
- The chicks avoid the middle and go to the sides of the house, resulting in damp litter.
- Reduce the underpressure.

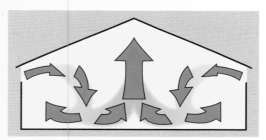

- The fresh cold air sinks too quickly and is therefore not being heated up enough.
  The chicks keep to the outermost parts and the middle of the house.
- This has created two empty strips down the length of the house: a zebra crossing effect.
- Increase the underpressure.

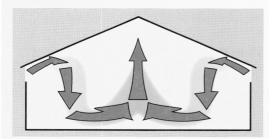

- The chicks move away from the edges and are mainly in the middle.
- The flaps are too tightly shut so there is too little air entering through each flap which dissipates too quickly.
- Open some of the flaps about two fingers more.

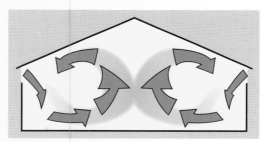

- In hot weather the flaps will turn.
- The air will pass right over the chicks at high velocity.
- This will make the air feel quite cool near the birds (wind chill effect). This should only be done deliberately if the ambient temperature is very high.

Source: Henk Rodenboog

Assessing your birds

Assess individual chicks regularly to get an impression of the flock. Automatic weighing will give you an idea of their average growth. If you pick up a couple of birds, you can learn more about the differences in weight and condition. However, it is important to take a good sample. How do the chicks react when you walk through them? If some chicks stay on the ground or sit down again quickly after being chased away, there is something wrong: the house is too warm, they have joint, tendon or bone pain, stomach pain caused by coccidiosis, weakness caused by dysbacteriosis or foot ulcers.

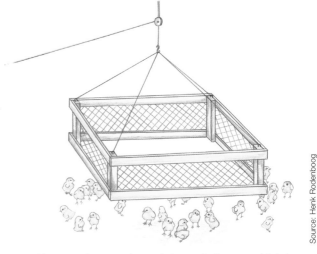

You can take a good sample by enclosing some birds in a frame. Use a raisable one to avoid dragging or chasing the chicks. Install one permanently in one or two strategic places in the house. This produces a better sample and you will always be weighing and assessing chicks in the same place.

Weight

You can determine the weight of the roosters and hens separately. Otherwise you will end up with a higher average weight if you weigh more roosters than hens. The difference is greater with older chicks: 16 per cent at 35 days. The more chicks you weigh, the better your result will be.

Abattoir report: useful information!

A poultry farmer not only needs to take note of the signals from his birds but also those he receives from the abattoir. The information in the slaughter report can tell you what needs to be improved, such as the number of chicks that arrived dead, rejections, haemorrhaging, scratches/injuries, hock burns, and so on. To see what can be improved, you can view abattoir reports in graph form for each part of successive flocks.

If you lift up a chick by the wings, its feet should point downwards. The chick on the right is holding its feet up, which could be early signs of stomach pain.

Footpads

The quality of the chick's footpad is an important indicator of litter quality. The drier and looser the litter, the less chance there is of footpad problems. Footpad lesions are painful and therefore bad for the welfare of the birds. They also cost you money, because chicks with affected feet seek out less feed and water, grow less and have lower feed conversion rates. There are also other possible causes: composition of the feed (and therefore of the manure) and differences between breeds.

What to do about footpad problems

- Provide dry litter. Use a different type of litter, such as maize silage. This will also reduce ammonia emissions. Avoid too high relative humidity, shorten the dark period, provide even lighting and adjust the ventilation in a high occupancy house. Consider a mobile feeding and drinking system for greater distribution of manure production.
- Make sure not too much drinking water is spilt. Use nipples with drip trays instead of cups and adjust the water pressure and water level properly.
- Talk to your feed supplier about the feed composition if the manure is on the thin side.
- Choose a breed that grows more slowly or slow down growth by reducing the protein content.

You can do this by adding more wheat.

Breast and hock irritations

Chicks that lie down a lot suffer from fewer footpad problems but are more affected by hock and breast irritations (breast blisters) than chicks that stand more.

Breast irritation

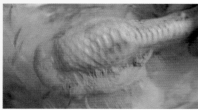

Hock irritation

Calculate your flock's footpad score.

Assess the feet of 100 birds to decide whether you need to take action.
Use the scoring system below.

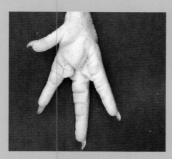

Score 0
Healthy foot.
No lesions or very few surface papillae affected.

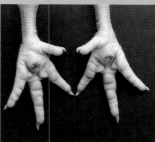

Score 1
Slightly abnormal. Few affected papillae or slight red discolouration; skin not deeply affected.

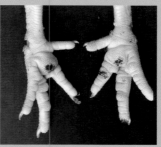

Score 2
Seriously affected. Large areas of affected papillae, skin more deeply affected. Wounds and infections also score 2.

Use the following formula:
(number of birds with score 1 x 0.5) +
(number of birds with score 2 x 2)

Explanation
< 50 points : no significant problems
50 – 80 points : moderate problems. Action required.
> 80 points : serious problem.
Urgent action required.

Source: C. Berg

Scratches on thighs

Are there any chicks with scratches on their thighs at the feeding line? These may well have had foot problems and were not able to get moving quickly enough when feeding started. They were trampled on, which caused these scratches. Other possible causes are too severe lighting programmes, too high density of chicks or too few feeding pans.

Signals from manure

Fresh manure can tell you a lot. A healthy, well-fed and well cared-for chick produces manure in neat pellets. Assess normal (intestinal) droppings and caecal droppings separately.

Manure not right

Digestion is below par. There are various reasons for this:

● Too much protein or a lot of potassium-rich protein products in the feed.
● Intestinal problems caused by abnormal gut flora in combination with coccidiosis, clostridium, E. coli etc.
● Virus infections.

Consult a vet for the right diagnosis.

Scores for intestinal droppings

You can pick up and roll a good pellet in your hand. That does not apply to caecal droppings, of course. If the manure is not in neat pellet form, the chicks are cold, they are sickening or the feed is wrong. Roughly speaking, the quality of the manure can be assessed as follows:

Right

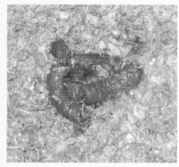

Reasonable

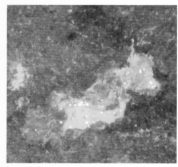

Not right

Source: A. Slaats

Scores for caecal droppings

Caecal droppings should be dark brown and not thin but sticky. If the caecal droppings turn lighter in colour, digestion is not optimal and there are too many nutrients remaining at the end of the small intestine. These will ferment in the caecum and will cause overly thin caecal droppings.

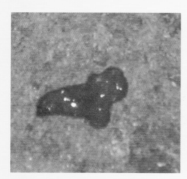

Right

Reasonable

Not right

Source: A. Slaats

Poor litter

Locally poor litter

When the chicks are 11 days old, the litter will become damp and it will feel warm from being warmed up by the chicks. If it becomes damp before then, the litter temperature is too low or the drinking water system is not working properly (it is leaking or spilling). In places where the litter is damp or which are avoided by chicks, there will be no heating effect and the floor will be cold. Chicks will avoid those places even more and condensation will cause the litter to deteriorate further.

If you see poor quality litter under the lamps, that means that the **light intensity** varies too much throughout the house. The difference in light intensity should be no more than a factor of 2. Chicks avoid places with too much light from above, the litter cools down and condensation occurs. Once this starts to happen, the problem gets constantly worse. Remove wet areas of litter. If dimming the light doesn't help, cover over the underside of the lamps. If you can't do so in the current cycle, opt for the definitive solution next time: once the house is empty, redistribute the lamps or install new HF lamps.

If you can clearly see entire strips of poor litter, this is often caused by poor **air movement**. The distribution of the birds therefore has a direct impact on the litter quality, and vice versa.

Wet litter everywhere

If all the litter gets wet, this can have various causes:

- Poor feed composition, making the manure too wet;
- Cold litter, causing condensation;
- Inadequate ventilation;
- Sick chicks (producing wet manure);
- Nights too long. The chicks are lying on the litter for too long periods at a time.

The litter should always be dry and slightly loose. It should not stick to your hands or boots too much. The litter in this photograph is good. From week 3, make a note of the quality of the litter in different parts of the house once a week, marking it on a map of the house, for example.

Wet manure?

Pick up a pellet and squeeze it. In this photo you can see that the pellet contains water. When you squeeze it, it drips: this is not right.

LOOK-THINK-ACT

What do you notice about the distribution of the chicks?

The chicks are avoiding certain parts, so there are empty strips. The chicks are doing this because the airflow is cold or the litter or light distribution is poor. Try to rectify this before the litter in those strips gets too wet.

Feed signals

Flying start

Right from day 1, it is important that **all chicks** start eating and drinking. Chicks that are unfit or cold will not eat but will stay sitting or will huddle together. This is a poor start and can result in an uneven flock. You can avoid this by providing warm litter (35-37°C or a floor temperature of > 28°C). You can further reduce the problem by feeding the chicks on the floor plates or on the paper for longer.

Feed too coarse or too fine

Chicks learn quickly, but they are also creatures of habit. Healthy chicks definitely prefer coarse particles, so fine feed tends to accumulate in the pans. Sometimes they actively seek out the fine feed. A preference for fine feed can often be an indication of health problems.

Eat up!

Don't let broiler chicks get too fussy. When they are a week old, allow them to finish the contents of the pans completely at a set time each day. Don't leave the pans empty for longer than one hour, otherwise it will have the effect of restricting feeding.

A set rhythm is reassuring and reduces the risk of pathogens forming in accumulated feed in the feed pan.

Abnormal behaviour

If the chicks are pecking up against the wall a lot and feed intake is low, this is often an indication that the chicks are lacking something. It can be a sign of an intestinal condition or something to do with the feed composition.

Picky eaters

Sometimes the chicks will throw the grain or the pellets or both out of the pan. There are two possible causes for this: pellets too hard and dry, or intestinal disorders. Providing too much or too little wheat in relation to the supplementary feed can also cause the birds to feed selectively. Intestinal disorders such as coccidiosis and dysbacteriosis can also result in selective feeding.

Drinking

Chicks need to be able to drink easily. Otherwise they will drink too little, eat too little and they won't grow properly.

Height of the nipples:

One cause of chicks drinking too little is that the nipples are too high or too low. Change the height and see whether this affects their water consumption.

Relationship between feed and water intake

Water intake depends on feed intake, feed composition, house temperature and age. As a rule of thumb, from 10 days the ratio between water and feed should be 1.7. Record the daily water and feed intake. A sudden change in water intake could be a signal that there is a health problem, disease or vaccination reaction. See whether the change coincides with a feed supply or a change in the feeding phase. Check the water pressure too.

What is the right drinking position?

The right drinking position is upright with the head up so that the water runs into the throat. What is upright? You can control this by raising or lowering the drinking nipples.

Source: Aviagen

For one week old chicks, the angle between the beak and the nipple should be 35-45°.

For chicks older than one week, the angle between the beak and the nipple should be 80-85°.

Water output from the nipples

If there is too little water coming out of the nipples, the chicks will drink too little. Check the water pressure and the water output from the nipples regularly. You can assess the flow speed by holding up a container to a nipple for one minute. Measure the amount of water in the container. Do this at several different drinking lines. A handy rule of thumb for the flow rate is the age of the chicks in days plus 20 ml/min. For example: 35 days + 20 = 55 ml/minute. Too much water will cause spillage and bad litter quality, which will in turn lead to poorer quality chicks and footpad lesions. Have the drinking water checked by a laboratory.
Check the drinking lines visually for soiling. Do this on the inside and outside of the system.

Source: B. Lott

LOOK-THINK-ACT

Dry litter = good litter?

What do you think of the litter in this picture? You can see that there are particles fluttering down to the ground. This is a good sign because it means that the litter is dry. However, litter always gets slightly wet from leaking nipples and spills. If the litter is too dry, this might be a sign that the chicks are not drinking enough. Check the water intake and if necessary the water output from the nipples all over the house.

Weak chicks

Most losses usually occur in the first seven days. If there is a problem with the quality of the mother birds or the hatching conditions, mortality rates can mount up. Good care is all the more important for weak chicks: enough feed and water that they can access easily. Keep them somewhere that has been warmed up well in advance and that has a well insulated floor (poultry paper or thick litter) with the temperature on the high side. Young chicks cannot regulate their own body temperature, and if they are not yet eating they will get cold and die.

Signal	Possible cause
Poorly developed birds	Difficulty finding feed and/or water. The vet could not be contacted easily or the feed on the paper was eaten up too quickly. This kind of problem cannot be fixed in this cycle.
Wrynecks and stargazers	Inflammation of the brain. This can be caused by a salmonella, streptococcal, enterococcal or fungal infection (Aspergillus fumigatus).
Lame chicks	Bacterial infection with salmonella, streptococcus, enterococcus or E. coli. A bacterial infection at this age is often related to the quality of the hatching eggs or conditions in the hatchery. Thereafter, the quality of care largely determines the severity of the problem.
Huddled up, feathers raised	The chicks are cold, possibly because of a bacterial infection.
Helicopter feathers	Malabsorption syndrome. This syndrome is the result of an early intestinal disorder in which the necessary ingredients are not absorbed by the bird in the correct proportions. Provide an extra boost with vitamins and minerals. You will have to disinfect thoroughly before the next cycle.

Wryneck resulting from meningitis.

Stargazer, also resulting from meningitis.

A 'helicopter' chicken can be identified by the poor feather development: down and feathers mixed up and pointing in all directions.

Vent pasting

A chick with whitish grey pasting round the vent. This is often caused by a serious bacterial infection (e.g. Salmonella) or a viral kidney disorder. These chicks should ideally be removed. An inflammation of the peritoneum affects intestinal peristalsis, which causes the urine to run spontaneously out of the vent. Once dried, it forms a cement-like coating.

A chick with a dark-grey 'pencil' formation is not so badly affected.

Identifying causes of death

In the event of mortality, the first thing to do is to determine what level of losses you have. But also check whether the dead birds are from particular places in the house. Are they mainly hens or roosters? Could the deaths be described as sudden? Also observe how a dead chick is lying; this can be an indication of the cause of the death, although this proof is far from watertight.

This can only be done with an autopsy.

Sudden (acute) deaths?

With sudden death, the dead chick is in excellent condition and has a full crop. You can recognise birds that die a non-acute death from disease by their reduced muscle mass, small, shrunken comb and dried out skin, particularly visible on the feet.

Characteristics of dead chicks	Possible cause
On the stomach or back	Metabolic disorder. Happens mainly between two and five weeks. Try to resolve the problem with feed management.
On the back with wings splayed and often with one foot in the air	Sudden death syndrome (flip-over). The young chick's heart stops, it jumps up into the air and falls down dead on its back or sometimes its stomach. Slow down growth slightly with lower light intensity until the loss rate is below 0.05% per day.
Well developed, with full crop	Chicks that die suddenly at an older age are suffering from excessive strain on the heart as a result of poor blood circulation. Another cause can be an inflammation of the heart wall or valve (endocarditis). Some chicks appear to be lame. A plug of inflamed material has become detached and wedged in a foot artery, for example. The foot feels cold to the touch. Some broiler farmers see sudden death as a sign of a good flock, but chicks that die in this way can't be explained to the consumer.
Moderate to poor condition, stomach full of liquid	Ascites. Ascites occurs from three weeks. Check the carbon dioxide level in the house. These chicks are more susceptible to heat stress. To avoid this problem in a subsequent cycle, restrict growth, make sure that animals are not too cold or reduce the temperature less quickly.
On the stomach, neck forward and feet back	Choking. These birds have been choked by a plug of inflamed material in the top of the respiratory tract as a result of a virus infection or a severe reaction to a vaccination. Another possible cause is a fungal infection: the birds gasp silently for air.
Seal position: on the stomach, feet back, neck stretched, beak slightly open and often with a morsel of litter in the beak	Botulism. This is rare. It can occur from two weeks. It can also be caused by an overdose of certain ionophoric anticoccidial agents and by enteritis with tissue necrosis (Clostridium).

The stomach of a chick suffering from ascites is filled with liquid.

A bird that has choked and died of a viral infection or too severe reaction to vaccination.

This bird has died of sudden death syndrome.

Broiler parent birds

Broiler parent birds are bred for growth and meat development, but they also have to lay eggs, and the eggs have to be fertilised. Because of the difference in breeding direction, broiler parent birds have different requirements for housing and care than laying hens or laying parent birds. If there are production problems, the cause will be found with the hens. If there are fertilisation and hatching problems, the causes will lie with both the roosters and the hens.

Rearing

Good uniformity within a flock of parent birds is essential for good production and fertilisation. Poor uniformity in weight and development can have different causes such as inadequate feeder length, too high bird density, poor distribution of feed, poor health etc.

Because the feed intake of broiler parent birds is highly restricted during the rearing period, there is always a run on the feeder at feeding times. Immediately after giving the feed, all birds must be eating. If there are animals running back and forth or clambering over other animals, the feeder is not long enough or it is difficult to access.

The practice of feed restriction, which is strictly speaking undesirable, plays a very minor role with slow-growing types.

Laying period

Feed intake is restricted less during the production period than during rearing. Nonetheless, you can't always ensure that all birds get enough to eat after transferring to the laying house.

This is because they were used to eating quickly during rearing. Make sure they can all eat at the same time. There must be feed everywhere within three minutes. If this is not possible, provide more feed hoppers, use a different feeding system or feed from the middle of the house.

How can you be sure that the roosters aren't getting too much or too little food? Measure the height of the rooster feeding line. First feed the hens, then the roosters a few minutes later. Check whether the roosters are able to access their feeders easily or whether a lot of roosters are also feeding with the hens.

The best way to check whether the roosters are eating enough is to weigh them every week. This is the only way you can find out their weights and distribution.

Difference in plumage caused by difference in occupancy

There are 12 rearing hens per square metre in the picture on the left and 8-9 on the right. But they have the same number of feeding points, so there is more competition. The hens in the picture on the left therefore have poorer plumage.

A good rooster is not fat

If a rooster looks too good, that could be a sign that he isn't mating regularly or properly. Pick up a rooster regularly during your inspection of the house. Roosters that are mating actively will have a damp vent surrounded by red skin. A rooster with a dry vent is not mating often or at all. A slightly bald breast and broken, raw feathers are a good sign on a rooster: a lot of nice down feathers are not.
A couple of hours before the light goes off, the roosters should be actively going about their business. A rooster that is not yet mating at 30 weeks will not start and can be removed.

Reaching sexual maturity together

If the roosters reach maturity earlier than the hens, the frightened hens will run away from pairing attempts. Roosters that reach maturity late run the risk of the hens dominating them so they are too scared to mate. This 'psychological castration' cannot be reversed.

Wounded hens

Wounds on sides are caused by deformed or untreated toes on the roosters and sexing mistakes (hens that look like roosters). Eliminate the sexing mistakes and roosters with deformed toes. Wounds can also be caused by having too many roosters or by hens clambering over each other.

Feeding roosters

A rooster that loses weight during the production period will start to moult and can't fertilise eggs. Make sure all roosters feed at the same time and keep hens away from the feeding roosters as much as possible. If not all roosters are feeding simultaneously, check that there is enough space for them all. Are some roosters too afraid to feed with the others? Is the feeding system properly suspended? Check the feeding system and the weights of the roosters.

Litter quality and fertilisation

Poor litter causes footpad problems. A rooster with sore feet will find it painful to mount the hens. That is bad for fertilisation. Make sure the litter is good quality and remove any lumps in the litter.

Right: moist vent, red breast skin and worn breast feathers.

The difference in physical condition is also indicated internally: testicle sizes of two roosters of the same age (42 weeks). The testicles on the left are the ideal size; those on the right are not.

The hens are sitting on the slats to escape mating: they are staying away from the roosters in the scratching area. There are too many amorous roosters, or the roosters reached sexual maturity a while before the hens.

Remove roosters with deformed toes because they can cause serious injury to the hens' flanks.

CHAPTER 6

Health

A chicken can only perform optimally if it is healthy. Sick animals have less desire to eat and drink even though they need extra energy to boost their natural defences. Producing proteins for growth and egg production therefore takes a back seat as survival is their priority. Consumption of trace elements and vitamins increases in diseased birds.

Don't only call the vet if there is a problem, but also to keep your finger on the pulse and make other arrangements before something goes wrong.

Disease always costs money. Besides the cost of lower production (growth, eggs, development) you also have to pay for the treatments: the direct cost of the drugs used and the indirect cost of waiting for drug residues to disappear from meat and eggs.

Unsaleable eggs are one of the costs of disease.

Disease signals

Diseases always manifest themselves in symptoms, and Poultry Signals are perfect for this. Identifying a disease therefore starts by being able to assess health properly. As soon as you have a good image of a healthy chicken in your mind, it is easier to pick up on subtle changes (see also chapter 1). So start with the disease signal: what does it tell you, and what is causing it? Use your senses: look, listen, smell and feel.

Categorising diseases

As soon as you identify a symptom, categorise it in a main group. This makes it easier to make a diagnosis because you can often rule out a number of diseases.

Signals that can help you identify symptoms are:
- the gastrointestinal system
- the breathing organs
- the laying organs (egg production)
- the musculoskeletal and nervous system.
- the skin and plumage

There are also acute diseases with a high mortality rate.

One size doesn't fit all

Symptoms of disease: hunched up, eyes shut, feathers fluffed out.

The annoying thing is that one symptom doesn't always lead you straight to a particular cause. You need to recognise several signals to be able to identify a disease. Conversely, you may also find that one disease can have various symptoms, so it may not be easy to narrow down.

Besides their main symptom, respiratory problems, diseases like avian flu and Newcastle disease can also cause lameness and diarrhoea, so they fit into several different groups.

Disease signals in pictures

This rearing hen is breathing through its open beak because of a respiratory inflammation.

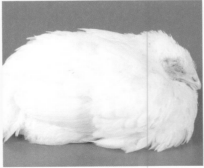

This broiler mother bird is lying hunched up with raised feathers. Her eyes are shut, she is taking virtually no notice of her surroundings and she does not get up to feed. She is very poorly.

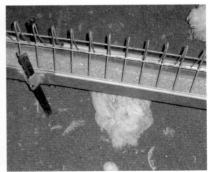

Sick birds tend to hide.

Biosecurity outside the house

Biosecurity is about keeping poultry healthy. First and foremost, disease must be kept outside the door: external biosecurity. Pay sufficient attention to routes along which infection can take place, and draw up a hygiene plan in which you list all activities and their frequency and order. Aspects that should always be included in the plan are rules for visitors and outside vehicles entering the premises, delivery and removal of animals, removal of sick animals and carcasses, use of boots and clothing, refilling the disinfection tank, cleaning, disinfection and pest control.

An effective layout

A well-designed layout with a clean and dirty access route is the basis for good external biosecurity. Only allow clean vehicles to enter the premises via the clean route. Enable unloading to take place via the dirty route, for example for feed trucks, so that they do not have to drive up to the house. Germs are very easily transmitted on shoes, clothes and hands and are then transferred to the hair and the airways. People who have to enter the house must always do so via the compulsory decontamination area.

Prevent young hens from bringing red mites into the laying farm by switching on the main lighting half an hour before capturing them. The lice will then leave the chicken. Just before capturing the chickens, switch the main lighting off and the blue replacement lighting on.

Decontamination area

The only access to the house must be through a decontamination area. In the clean area, visitors wash their hands or shower, if facilities exist. They then put on clean protective clothing and boots and can then proceed into the house. When the visitors leave the house, the boots are removed and cleaned. The visitors remove the protective clothing, change back into their own clothes and leave the decontamination area on the 'dirty side'.

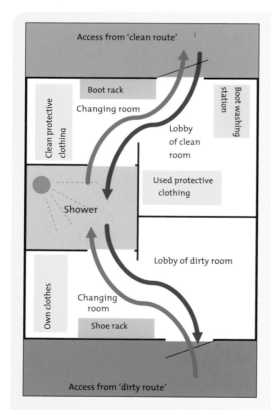

Ideal situation: room with two doors, separate place for dirty and clean clothing and boots, possibly showers

Bad situation: dirty and clean people crossing over the same bench, and dirty and clean clothes hanging on the same hooks.

Biosecurity in the house

Also avoid spreading diseases in the house itself: internal biosecurity. Take a critical look at your own working methods. How clean are your overalls and boots? There are potential pathogens in the manure and dust you carry around with you. What route do you take when you walk round the house? Always walk from the area with the youngest birds to the area with the oldest ones. Do you always make sure you go from clean to dirty, and do you wash your hands and change your clothing or boots when you go to a different section or house? Don't allow affected or sick birds to run around: always remove them.

What is your vermin situation? Vermin are a major transmitter of diseases. So it is essential to protect against and control vermin. The level of biosecurity you should aim for partly depends on the husbandry system you use. Very strict measures are pretty pointless in free range systems, for example. Don't forget to check your fan outlets. Make sure they don't blow straight into another house.

Remove dead birds

Remove dead birds daily and do not allow them to pile up next to the house door. Place them in a refrigerated carcass storage facility. Check the laying nests, slats and litter every day. Make sure everything is easy to see and easily accessible.

Dead animals are a breeding ground for bacteria. Hens peck at dead birds, spreading bacteria fast among the flock.

Controlling mice and rats

Mice and rats are wary transmitters of disease, including salmonella:
- Seal holes in floors and walls and cracks or chinks in buildings, windows and doors.
- Remove feed, manure and egg residues wherever possible and tidy up rubbish promptly.
- Don't use anterooms or lofts as storage spaces.
- Store things in closed rooms.

It is impossible to keep a farm entirely free of rats and mice. So remain alert and check the house regularly for traces of rats and mice. Set up mousetraps and bait boxes with poison.
Ideally you should bring in a specialist company to perform regular and effective vermin control.

Make sure that there are no places where mice can hide, for example by keeping the first few metres around the house free from vegetation. Grass is fine, but keep it short.

Controlling flies

Make sure that the manure remains sufficiently dry (> 45% dry matter) as fly larvae thrive in wet manure. Remove the manure regularly, particularly in the summer months. Always install UV fly killers in the house and count the adult flies that land on it at set times. If the number increases noticeably, there is a breeding ground with larvae and maggots somewhere. Find the source and treat it immediately with larvae killer. Besides chemical agents, these days you can also use a biological method with predator flies.

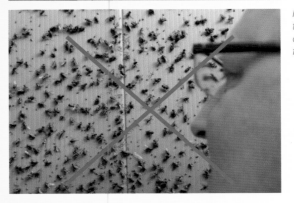

Flies spread germs when they are eaten by the chickens, via hair and in faeces.

What seems to be the trouble?

When assessing a flock, there are three key questions:

1. What am I observing? Observing is not just looking, but also listening, smelling and feeling. The symptoms, a disease profile.
2. What has caused it? The diagnosis.
3. What can I do about it? What action do I need to take? Treatment and prevention.

Also ask yourself whether the problem is in the whole flock or just in an individual bird.

How to perform a clinical examination

Step 1 Medical history
- What are the symptoms?
- When did the problems start?
- Do you have the results of any previous examinations?
- Have these problems been going on for some time on the farm, or have they occurred before?
- What are the technical characteristics?

Step 2 Looking at the birds
- When assessing several houses or flocks, always look at the healthy ones first, followed by the sick ones, and then look from young to old.
- Assess the flock as a whole: are there noticeable symptoms? If so, how many animals show symptoms and how serious are these? How is the uniformity, the distribution in the poultry house and behaviour? What can you tell, for example, by the plumage, feathers in the barn and digestion of the manure?
- Perform a physical (clinical) examination of any abnormal or sick birds.
- Assess the external and internal egg quality.

Step 3 Further examination
What additional examinations are needed to establish the cause? Take the time to select the right birds for this examination and send in enough birds and/or samples. Possibilities are:
- Autopsy of sick birds and follow up examination of organ samples (bacteriological, virological, parasite). Depending on the problem, your vet may tell you to send in sick birds, and in some cases healthy ones too, for the following examinations:
- Examination of paired blood samples (samples taken on appearance of symptoms and three weeks later)
- Examination of other sample material such as windpipe swabs and manure
- Examination of the house climate.

Step 4 Additional laboratory tests.
These may sometimes be necessary in order to obtain a definitive diagnosis.

Step 5 Recommendations for other and subsequent flocks.

Gastrointestinal problems

In birds, the vent, or cloaca (Latin for 'sewer'), is not only the place where solid waste is excreted, but also waste products from the kidneys. Hens and roosters also excrete something else here: the egg and sperm respectively.

Three different types of manure/waste products can be distinguished:

1. Normal intestinal droppings, the voluminous ones which are often comma-shaped. When normal, the surface is covered in very small cracks and the droppings remain dry when squeezed.

2. Caecal droppings. In the mornings chickens deposit a sticky, damp, shiny pile which ranges from caramel to chocolate brown in colour.

3. Urates from the kidneys. Birds do not urinate like mammals (they have no bladder) but convert their urine into uric acid crystals which are deposited in a white layer on the droppings.

Besides abnormal manure, there are other general indications of gastrointestinal problems: huddling together, fluffed up feathers, lethargy and death. Birds with digestive problems have too little energy and therefore have a greater need for warmth. Increase the house temperature for a while. Chronic digestive problems can lead to deficiencies of proteins, vitamins, minerals and trace elements.

Left: intestinal droppings with caecal droppings on top, right: caecal droppings

Abnormal droppings and possible causes

Signal	Possible cause
Homogenously thin	Intestinal problem
Pool of water with strings of urates and clumps of droppings	Some virus infections (such as Gumboro and renal IB)
Feed components visible:	Poor digestion
orange-red, sticky strings	Too long without food, or intestine affected by e.g. coccidiosis
Fresh blood in stools	Possibilities include coccidiosis (especially caecal coccidiosis)
Dark green droppings	Loss of appetite or severe acute diarrhoea with undigested bile salts
Thin yellow caecal droppings with gas formation	Intestinal dysfunction or incorrect feeding
Watery, white droppings	Kidney problem or inadequate feeding resulting from infection

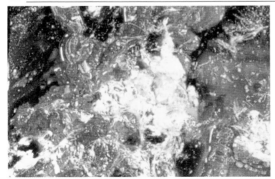
Large amounts of watery, white excreta from the kidneys: renal IB or Gumboro

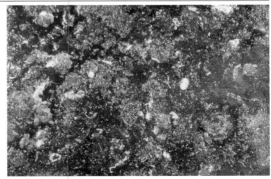
Fresh blood in the droppings comes from the intestinal tract and indicates acute caecal coccidiosis.

Respiratory diseases

Chickens suffering from respiratory diseases will be short of breath and often breathe through their open beaks. But this can also be an indication of problems with the house climate, fever, pain and anaemia.

Signals of respiratory problems

Signals that are specific to respiratory problems:

- Unusual breathing noise: sniffing, snuffling and snorting, rattling or hawking, crying, yawning and screeching. The best time to observe this is when the chickens are at rest (e.g. in the evening when it is dark);

Many respiratory problems start with a slight inflammation of the eye membrane, which can be recognised by slight foaming in the corner of the eye.

Short of breath, but no unusual noises. These chickens have a fungal infection of the lungs.

Action needed: this hen has a serious eye membrane inflammation, and its sinuses below the eyes are swollen.

- Shortness of breath: animals breathe through the open beak and make pumping movements with the abdominal muscles;
- Inflammation of the eye membrane (wet or thick eyes), nasal cavity and pharynx;
- Enlarged heads from swelling of the sinuses.

There are also some less specific signals: sitting huddled together, fluffed up feathers, lethargy and death.

Signals of climate problems

If the house is too hot, chickens will seek out cooler spots; they will sit huddled together along the walls, for example. They will often sit with beaks open and necks stretched. Their wings will hang loose against the body and their tail will bob up and down. But you won't hear any noise. The comb and wattles are dark red. Birds at risk of suffocating lie on the ground with feet pointing backwards and necks stretched.

Signals of fever

The normal body temperature of a fully grown chicken varies between 40.6 and 41.7°C. Chickens can develop a fever from bacterial and viral infections. This is most noticeable with Gumboro and IB. Because the birds are sick, they will huddle together so they can't bring down their temperature. They will then die from overheating and their feet will lie stiff against their bodies. If you open one up just after it has died, steam will escape: their body temperature may have increased to as much as 45°C!

Pain signals

Sitting with the beak open can also be a sign of severe pain in a bird. This is most obvious in turkeys, but you also see it in broilers. Adult hens express pain much less clearly.

Anaemia signals

Chickens sometimes seem to have difficulty breathing because of a respiratory problem, but on closer examination they may be found to be suffering from severe anaemia caused by a serious louse infection, for example.

Related signals

In the early stages of respiratory problems, the signals are often the same and there is nothing to tell you whether the problem is mild or a serious, possibly notifiable disease. You can tell a lot from the other signals associated with respiratory problems. A poultry farmer should therefore always talk to his vet straight away if mortality increases or if production, feeding or drinking dwindles. Further laboratory tests will be needed to confirm the illness.

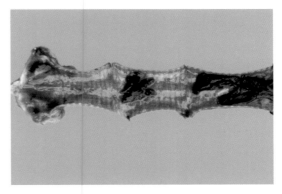

Red windpipe caused by infectious laryngotracheitis (ILT)

Sounds as a signal

Type of sound	Cause	Possible cause
No sound, beak open	No excessive mucus or inflammatory fluid in the airways	Fever, high house temperature, fungal infection on lungs or pain
Sniffing	Slight mucous membrane irritation with small amount of inflammatory fluid, moist eyes	Poor house climate: high ammonia, low relative humidity.
Snuffling and snorting	Mucous membrane irritation in upper airways, sometimes coupled with eye membrane inflammation	Vaccination reaction or start of viral infection. Viral or bacterial infection, vaccination reaction
Rattling or hawking	Mucous membrane irritation in nasal cavity and upper windpipe with excessive mucus formation	Poor house climate with E. coli If symptoms appear suddenly: IB or NCD
Squealing, yawning and screeching	Inflammation of the airways with stiff mucus, often sudden death from suffocating	AI, NCD, IB or ILT with E. coli

Clap your hands once or whistle loudly when you enter the poultry house. The chickens will stop in their tracks and you will be able to hear soft rattling and coughing (flock level).

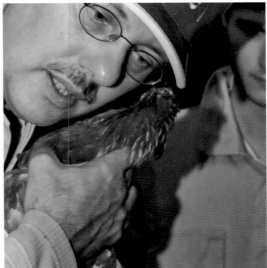

If you suspect an airway infection, hold up a chicken with the breast to your ear and listen and feel for any rattling or other unusual breathing (chicken level).

Egg production problems

Is the number of eggs produced consistently below standard, or is the quality of the eggs poor? Then this indicates a production problem. It is not only infections that can cause production problems. Production can get under way late because of a poor lighting programme, too little feed or even too much, or a too low body weight.
Poor flock uniformity caused by diseases during rearing, poor beak trimming or to strict feed restrictions can also result in a low production peak. If production is down, look out for other symptoms as well.
For more information on abnormal eggs, see also chapter 4.

Clinical examination

With many production problems, you will see little if anything wrong with the birds. But it is still important to have a good look at the flock and listen to it. If you can see any other disease symptoms, then it can be much easier to pinpoint a cause. Weigh your birds weekly so that you will notice any changes in their condition in good time.

Blood test

In the event of production problems, take blood samples from 24 birds from all over the house. Do this right at the beginning of the problems (acute stage) and 3 to 4 weeks later. During the three weeks after the infection, the birds will have formed antibodies which will show up in the blood.
The blood samples can be tested for antibodies against IB, EDS, TRT, Mycoplasma gallisepticum (Mg) and avian encephalomyelitis (epidemic tremor, AE).

Always test the blood

Check the initial status of all your flocks at the beginning of the laying period (at 20 to 22 weeks) with a blood test, or freeze blood serum to test for antibodies in the event of later problems.

If you are having production problems, also think about how the birds were reared. The hens may not have a uniform weight because of illness or vaccination reaction, for example. A non-uniform flock will get off to a non-uniform production start.

The egg on the left has calcium speckles which can have different causes.

Check points in case you have production problems

When investigating production problems at flock level, besides the obvious points, make sure you pay additional attention to the history of the production, the egg quality and the rearing period.

History
● Production curve (egg production, production peak, egg mass, persistency of production), mortality percentage, age at start of production or 50%-production point.

Egg quality
● Egg weight and uniformity (weight, size)
● Shell quality: shell colour and thickness, cracks and breaks, glassy tips, dirty shells, malformations: rings, asymmetry, pimples
● Internal egg quality: height of thick albumen (Haugh units), albumen and yolk colour
● Distribution of first and second grade eggs, characteristics of second grade eggs

Information on the rearing period
● Body weight and uniformity
● Transition from rearing to production period
● Vaccination schedule
● Autopsy reports (unfortunately, too few autopsies are performed on young hens in the rearing period)
● Lighting programme

Ridged shell

Pimples caused by infectious bronchitis

Causes of egg production problems

Drop in production	Other signals	Cause	Effect on eggshell	Impact on egg content
0	None	*Mycoplasma synoviae*	Glassy egg tips	-
0-15	Respiratory problems: sometimes slight, sometimes more serious caused by mixed infections	*Mycoplasma gallisepticum*	Possibly determined by additional infection	Possibly determined by additional infection
1-10	3-5% have puffy heads/noses	TRT	Pale shells	-
5-15	Reduced feed intake, respiratory complaints, wet manure due to kidney problems	Infectious Bronchitis*	Rings, pimples, asymmetric eggs	Watery albumen, loose air pocket, broken chalaza
10-90	Egg-binding, kidney problems, respiratory problems during rearing	Infectious Bronchitis during rearing**	Pale, weak shells, wind eggs, pimples, rings, asymmetric eggs	Watery albumen, loose air pocket, broken chalaza
5-20	Seriously short of breath, death	ILT	Pale shells	-
5-20	Poor feed intake	Feed quality	Varying	-
10	Rickets	Vit. D3 deficiency, Ca/P balance	Thin shells, wind eggs	-
10-60	No	Avian encephalomyelitis	No	-
30-50	No	Egg Drop Syndrome	Pale, weak shells, wind eggs	Cloudy albumen
10-100	Severely short of breath, diarrhoea, nervous symptoms, high mortality	Avian flu, Newcastle disease	Pale shells, wind eggs	Watery albumen, loose air pocket

* It is rare for all the signals and symptoms listed here to occur simultaneously in one flock.

** See remarks on IB. The consequences during the laying period are also associated with the age at which the IB infection occurred in the rearing period.

Locomotive organs disorders

The causes of locomotive problems can be traced back to the nervous system (brain and nerve bundles) or the musculoskeletal system (muscles, bones, joints). The former leads to lameness, wryneck and compulsive movements, such as with avian encephalomyelitis, vitamin E deficiency, Marek, AI and NCD.

Limping in one or both legs?

In limping birds, watch for symmetrical or asymmetrical limping. Asymmetrical limping can be caused by foot damage, a joint inflammation or Marek's disease. Symmetrical limping often indicates a more central cause such as Reovirus-induced tenosynovitis or bone pain.

Compared with the meat sector, foot problems such as Reovirus-induced tenosynovitis, perosis and hock tendon problems occur relatively infrequently in the laying sector. Bone pain from rapid osteoporosis can occur at any age. Specialist knowledge is needed to be able to interpret the degree of deterioration of the bone.

Footpad ulcers

Footpad ulcers mainly occur with broilers. In the first 14 days the skin on the feet is still thin; it only becomes callous later on. Uric acid and ammonia in wet poultry house affects the skin, causing cracking and inflammation. If the litter is wet when the bird is older, the footpads can become severely inflamed. If the footpads remain dry and clean for the first few weeks, the birds will be much less prone to footpad inflammation when they are older, even if the litter is in poor condition. See page 79 for more information.

The chicken on the left is lame in one foot: asymmetrical.

Footpad ulcer on a laying hen.

Motor disorder caused by a Reovirus-induced tenosynovitis infection.

Sudden increase in mortality

An increase in bird mortality, particularly if it happens suddenly, is always a major cause for alarm. Both the welfare of the flock and its production and therefore your financial result are seriously affected.

Be aware of when the alarm bells should start ringing. More than 0.1% mortality per day can be described as a significant increase. If the mortality rate is more than 0.5% per day, you are talking about a dramatic increase.

Possible causes

Infectious causes (germs)
- acute coccidiosis
- E. coli infection
- Erysipelothrix rhusiopathiae
- Avian Influenza (AI)
- Newcastle disease (ND)
- Gumboro disease
- necrotic enteritis (*Clostridium perfringens*)
- Salmonella
- fowl cholera (*Pasteurella multocida*)
- botulism

Non-infectious causes
- Power failure (ventilation failure)
- house climate related (heat stress; carbon monoxide poisoning; ventilation failure)
- stampeding/fright reaction
- water and feed disruptions
- toxicity (salt).

When losses occur, always check the surviving birds

Avoid ventilation errors. Check all your equipment at set times.

Always hand over carcasses on the public road. The carcass truck must not enter your 'clean' route. Carcasses must be chilled down to approximately 7°C in carcass bins to avoid unpleasant odours and the spread of germs.

Summary of the main diseases

A disease is relevant to commercial poultry if it occurs frequently and if an outbreak results in economic loss. Zoonoses - infections that can be transmitted from animal to man, such as Salmonella enteritidis and Erysipelas - are extremely important in terms of public health.

Viruses

Infectious bronchitis (IB)

The IB virus is very common. The first problems arise as early as 2 to 3 days after the virus has hit a flock, and it takes no time at all for the entire flock to be infected. Infected birds spread the IB virus for many weeks after recovery, and the virus can survive for months in the intestines. As soon as a symptom-free carrier is stressed, for example after transportation or other infections, the IB virus can re-emerge.

In young birds (particularly broilers) the IB virus results in respiratory problems, often followed by an E. coli infection. In layers you may often only notice production problems. In some cases the IB virus can even cause kidney complaints and digestive problems. The IB virus changes continuously, producing new variants all the time

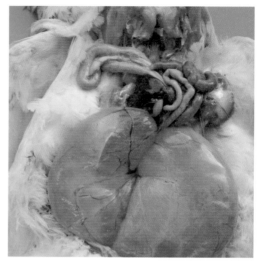

This egg-bound bird looks normal on the outside but can't lay an egg because her oviduct is deformed. The bird adopts a penguin stance.

Infectious laryngotracheitis (ILT)

ILT is a viral disease which causes severe breathing problems, loss of production and death. Brown layers and broiler parent birds, but also broilers, display particularly severe symptoms: serious breathing difficulties with a sometimes bloody nasal discharge. In the Netherlands, ILT is diagnosed no more than a few times per year.

Breathing difficulties

Egg Drop Syndrome (EDS)

EDS occurs occasionally, particularly in the first few months of production and with heavier breeds (Brown layers, broiler mother birds). Vaccination keeps the number of outbreaks limited. There is no treatment for EDS because it is caused by a virus. The disease spreads slowly: more quickly in non-caged systems than in caged systems. Typical of the infection are the large number of weak shells and wind eggs.

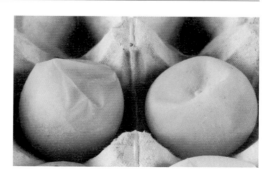

Wind egg caused by Egg Drop Syndrome

Viruses

Marek's disease

Marek's disease is a Herpes virus infection that causes tumours. It resides in the feather follicle cells and is therefore also found in dust particles from skin and feathers. Feather dust - and therefore potentially Marek's disease - can be found everywhere where chickens are or have been. So it is important to vaccinate chicks immediately after hatching and house them in a clean environment. You should also keep different aged chicks apart.

If inadequately protected chicks are infected in the first six to eight weeks of life, disease symptoms will emerge from about 15 weeks.

The disease has three forms:

Neurological: often asymmetrical lameness in the feet, for example

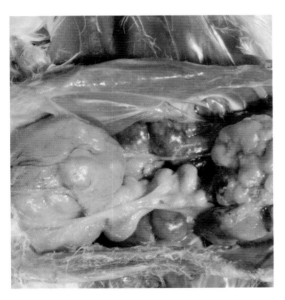

Visceral: tumours in internal organs

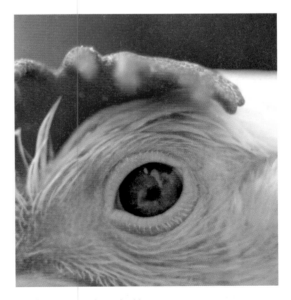

Ocular: grey, irregular iris

Viruses

Avian influenza (AI, a.k.a. bird flu or fowl pest)

Symptoms after infection with a high-pathogenic form of the AI virus are a sudden increase in mortality that suddenly rises again within a few days; swelling of the head, purple discolouration of the head, comb and wattles; subcutaneous haemorrhaging; shortness of breath; diarrhoea; lameness; huddling and ruffled feathers. The AI virus can therefore cause all kinds of symptoms, making it difficult to identify immediately. AI, NCD, ILT, TRT and sometimes IB can all produce similar symptoms. AI is notifiable.

AI, bird flu

Newcastle disease, ND (pseudo-fowl pest)

ND is not called pseudo-fowl pest for nothing. The symptoms of ND and AI are alike as two peas in a pod. ND is also notifiable and requires the same measures to be taken as for an AI outbreak. The ND virus is a paramyxovirus, while the AI virus is an orthomyxovirus. In the Netherlands, commercial poultry must be vaccinated against this by law. The effect of the vaccination must also be verified by means of a blood test.

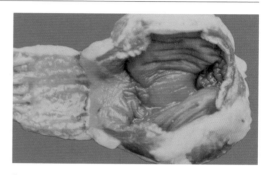

Proventricular bleeding

Gumboro disease

Gumboro is a serious viral disease that affects young chickens and can be accompanied by sudden death, typical watery, yellowy-white urate diarrhoea and reduced immunity. Rearing pullets are much more susceptible than broiler chicks, with mortality rates sometimes exceeding 50%: losses among broilers usually run to no more than between five and ten per cent.

Autopsy reveals typical abnormalities: the bursa is swollen and surrounded by a glassy skin (oedema), often with haemorrhaging. Muscle haemorrhaging and swollen kidneys complete the picture.

There is no treatment. Talk to your vet about the possibility of vaccinating subsequent flocks against Gumboro and at what age.

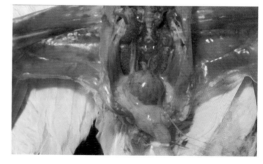

Inflamed bursa

Avian encephalomyelitis

Avian encephalomyelitis is a viral disease that causes lameness in young chicks, a significant drop in egg production of between 10 and 15% in layers and an approximately 5% drop in breeding results in parent birds. The virus is transmitted to progeny through the egg.

In pullets, around 15% (or anything up to 60%) display lameness (squatting, lying on the side) and tremors. The mortality rate among affected birds is 50%. The tremors are usually only seen or felt in a small number of birds by picking them up.

Typical lateral position caused by avian encephalomyelitis

Bacteria

Salmonellosis

Several Salmonella serotypes can cause sickness in poultry. Typical symptoms are diarrhoea and greatly increased mortality, particularly in the first and second week of life. Losses from peritoneal inflammation caused by S. enteritidis are sometimes observed in adult layers.

S. gallinarum results in widespread mortality, including in older birds. Autopsy reveals inflammation of internal organs including the ovaries and peritoneum.
Antibacterial treatments and vaccinations are ultimately ineffective.

In humans, some serotypes including S. enteritidis and S. typhimurium cause food poisoning.

Abnormal ovary with follicle stalk formation, commonly seen with an S. gallinarum infection

Dark, inflamed pericardium and swollen liver caused by S. enteritidis infection

E. coli or peritonitis

This is very common in adult hens: moderately to severely increased losses of birds in top condition are often the only symptom. Production is usually more or less unaffected. Sick birds are rare, and production is usually maintained.

In a flock of hens with colibacillosis, the birds will huddle together with raised feathers. Their breathing is laboured, they snort and cough and often produce thin droppings. There may be lame birds, and some birds may stop producing.

Losses are between 0.2 and 1% per day. Autopsy reveals inflamed air sacs, liver capsule and heart sac. Risk factors for colibacillosis are viral infections of the airways, poor house climate and inadequate hygiene.

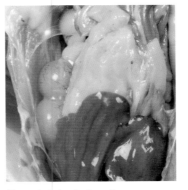

Normal abdominal cavity

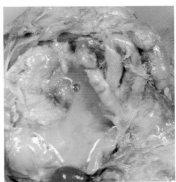

Peritonitis in a layer

Brachyspira infection

Brachyspira bacteria cause avian intestinal spirochaetosis (AIS), a chronic intestinal inflammation resulting in reduced nutrient intake. This causes deficiency and lower resistance. The symptoms include frequent drops in production, diarrhoea, weight loss and higher bird losses.

Foamy caecal content

Erysipelas

Erysipelas is caused by the bacterium *Erysipelothrix rhusiopathiae* and is particularly relevant to turkey and free range chicken farms. The bacteria can survive for many years in the ground, but also in carcasses.
Besides slightly lethargic, weak chickens, thin manure, higher mortality and a significant drop in production, there are very few typical symptoms.
The next flock can be vaccinated as a preventive measure.
Warning: Erysipelas is a zoonosis! Humans can be infected through skin wounds, producing local inflammation with a red, painful swelling.

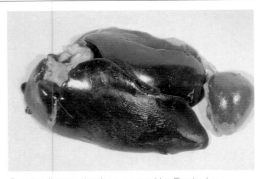

Swollen liver and spleen caused by Erysipelas

Bacteria

Mycoplasmosis
Mycoplasma gallisepticum (M.g.) infection mainly causes inflammation of the breathing organs in chicks. Older birds also suffer from production problems. The infection is a chronic lifelong condition.

Swollen head caused by mycoplasmosis

Fowl cholera (*Pasteurella multocida*)
Fowl cholera has an acute and a chronic form and is caused by the Pasteurella multocida bacterium. The acute form is associated mainly with higher mortality and diarrhoea. The chronic form can result in inflammation of the comb and wattles. Fowl cholera can be a serious problem in layers, turkeys and ducks, and the bacteria are also found in other wild birds and even in rats, mice and pigs. Options are preventative vaccination and antibiotic treatment.

Swollen comb and wattles caused by Pasteurella multocida.

Cause unknown

Chronic enteritis
Chronic enteritis often occurs at around 25 weeks when production is increasing fast. The first symptoms are distress, thin manure, reduced feed intake, poor production increase, messy plumage and loss of feathers which are subsequently eaten. Autopsy reveals a clear intestinal disorder in the first 20-30 cm of the intestine (the duodenum), i.e. too much and too thin content with an abnormal colour. There may also often be small necrotic lesions caused by Clostridium spp. These lesions are dark-grey in colour, sometimes with obvious bleeding. The irritated intestinal mucous membrane tries to repair itself by renewing more rapidly but is then unable to mature properly. This causes digestive problems and changes the composition of the gut contents. The changed gut contents form a breeding ground for bacteria that do not belong in the first part of the gut and lead to further irritation, making the enteritis chronic.

Chronic enteritis is best treated by improving the gut function and suppressing the irritating gut bacteria. This can partly be controlled via the feed and with additives, like copper sulphate.

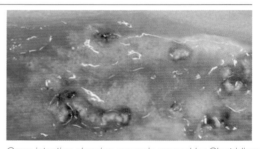

Open intestine showing necrosis caused by Clostridium.

Untidy plumage: signal of chronic enteritis

Gut parasites

Coccidiosis

Coccidiosis is caused by several types of Eimeria. This single-cell gut parasite is common in poultry and causes very minor to severe harm to the gut. Moderate infections can result in subclinical disease, while mass infection can lead to clinical symptoms such as diarrhoea and sometimes death. Coccidia spread as oocysts which are difficult to destroy with disinfectants. Coccidioses is very widely spread and, accordingly, is one of the most harmful diseases in poultry keeping.

The severity of the symptoms depends on the species of Eimeria: from slightly retarded growth with E. acervulina infection to sudden death with E. necatrix or E. brunetti infection. The manure is often abnormal. With caecal coccidiosis there may be fresh blood in the droppings. Coccidiosis can also lead to bacterial enteritis. In broilers, the main bacteria are E. acervulina, E. maxima, E. tenella, E. mitis and E. praecox. Relevant to older birds are also E. necatrix and E. brunetti.

Prevention

Good hygiene and good litter quality are essential for limiting harm from coccidiosis. **Vaccination** is possible with live vaccines: attenuated (low-virulence) or non-attenuated (wild type) strains. Such a vaccination is common with birds intended for reproduction, for layers in alternative systems and increasingly for broilers.

Most vaccines contain living coccidiostat-susceptible strains. This can also be a solution where broilers have developed multi-resistance to coccidiostats. They improve the effectiveness of these coccidiostats.

Coccidiostats are mixed into broiler feed as a preventive measure. Problems with the use of these products are greater resistance in the parasites if a particular product is used too long and cross-resistance between related products.

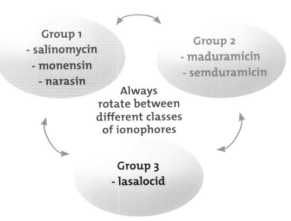

Greater resistance and cross-resistance can be overcome by rotating promptly between coccidiostats with different mechanisms of action.

There are five species of Eimeria with relevance to chickens. Each species has its own favourite spot in the gut

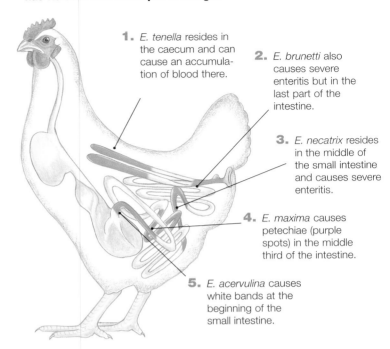

1. *E. tenella* resides in the caecum and can cause an accumulation of blood there.

2. *E. brunetti* also causes severe enteritis but in the last part of the intestine.

3. *E. necatrix* resides in the middle of the small intestine and causes severe enteritis.

4. *E. maxima* causes petechiae (purple spots) in the middle third of the intestine.

5. *E. acervulina* causes white bands at the beginning of the small intestine.

Pale bird suffering from caecal coccidiosis

The economic consequences are often underestimated: only the tip of the iceberg (clinical coccidiosis) is visible, but below that there lurks a much greater risk (subclinical coccidiosis).

Histomoniasis

Like Eimeria, Histomonas meleagridis is a single-celled parasite that can cause severe disease symptoms and death in chickens and turkeys. Autopsy reveals typical inflammations of the liver and caecum. There is no treatment. However, you can tackle the intermediate host (the caecal worm), which reduces the pressure of infection.

Histomonas causes typical lesions in the liver.

Worms

Worm egg count

To get a good impression of the worm infection in a flock, it is recommended to have a worm egg count performed every six weeks. To do this, take a mixed sample of 20 piles of intestinal droppings and 20 piles of caecal droppings.

Caecal droppings are sometimes mixed with the intestinal droppings, but if it is important to differentiate between the parasitic round-worm Ascaridia galli and the nematode parasite Heterakis gallinarum, collect the two kinds separately. The caecal worm resides in the caecum and the large roundworm in the small intestine. The droppings need to be as fresh as possible. The samples should be kept chilled and examined within a week.

Autopsy

If the worm egg count cannot distinguish between the types of worm, autopsy of some birds may be required:

- to establish whether the worm is a parasitic roundworm or a nematode parasite
- to rule out other infections with similar symptoms
- to determine the severity of the infection and the damage to the intestine.

Symptoms

- Usually a slow process, i.e. a chronic condition
- Sometimes slight diarrhoea, weight loss or retarded growth
- Hens 'dry out': comb shrinks, egg production ceases
- With persistent, severe infection: pale comb and wattles, exhaustion
- The disease generally becomes more severe in young birds than in older ones.

Worm eggs in the droppings. What now?

Depending on the type of worm and the number of faecal eggs per gram (EPG), it may be necessary to deworm the chickens:

- EPG >1000 of the large roundworm
- EPG > 10 of the hairworm
- in case of caecal worm infection, de-worming is not immediately necessary.

Also look at the production figures and the condition and health of the birds.

Severe large roundworm infection

Treatment

There are various ways of tackling worm problems:

- A strategy of deworming every six weeks to prevent a serious threat of infection. Every three weeks for caecal worm/tapeworm.
- A strategy of manure analysis every six weeks, with autopsy in case of doubt; possible treatment on that basis.
- Only deworm if worm infections are found by chance.

Large roundworm *(Ascaridia galli)*

Large round worm infections are often symptom-free. Death only occurs with severe infection, usually as a result of intestinal damage by larvae or blockage of the intestine. The severe symptoms are mainly seen around three weeks after infection.

Caecal worm *(Heterakis gallinarum)*

The caecal worm is not actually, or only very slightly, pathogenic but it can transmit the serious disease blackhead (histomonas) via the eggs. For treatment advice for worms, you will need to know whether they are large roundworms or caecal worms. The difference can only be ascertained by autopsy or by collecting intestinal and caecal droppings separately. You should do this if there is histomonas in the vicinity, for example.

Tapeworm *(Raillietina)*

The tapeworm is easy to recognise by its jointed structure. This worm damages the intestines. When a worm segment containing eggs is excreted via the manure, the eggs are eaten by beetles (including litter beetles) and ants. Chickens re-infect themselves by picking up these intermediate hosts. After about two weeks, more segments containing eggs are excreted and the cycle starts again.

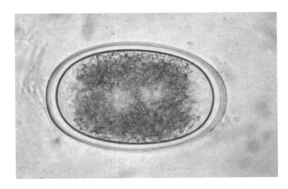

A ringworm egg

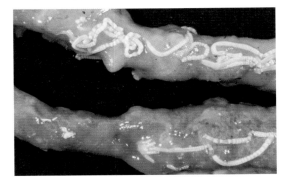

The tapeworm (Raillietina) is easy to recognise by its typical jointed structure and length.

Caecal worm

Red mites

Red mites can carry harmful bacteria or viruses. The bloodsucking parasite transfers them as it passes from one chicken to the next. With a severe red mite infection, chickens lose a lot of blood which can lead to anaemia, and in turn death. An average red mite infection reduces the chicken's resistance, but there are few external symptoms other than the fact that their plumage is rougher because they pick at the itchy skin. Chickens control red mites naturally by taking regular dust baths.

Accumulation of live mites on the egg belt: an ideal means of transport for eggs and mites.

Fighting the mite in an empty house

Red mites are easier to control when the house is empty. Clean it well to remove the hiding places such as under piles of manure. If you use pesticides, make sure you follow the instructions properly. A too low temperature can dramatically reduce the effectiveness of certain products. Heat treating the house can also greatly reduce an infection. Birds' nests on the outside of the house are a potential source of infection: remove them.

Pest control during an inspection

During an inspection, you need to act fast at places where the population manifests itself first. You can treat locally straightaway without having to treat the entire house, for example with silica powder or biodiesel. Another possibility is physiological control. This is a method in which the birds' blood is made unattractive to the red mite by feeding the chickens vitamin B2 or garlic. However, this is less effective with a severe infection. You need to start early.

Only mite-free hens

Make sure you obtain mite-free pullets if you have the choice.

LOOK-THINK-ACT

What does this behaviour tell you?

These hens are dust bathing. This can be seen by the stretched-out leg of the hen in the middle. Dust baths help to fight blood mites.

However, if you find the hens resting in the litter, it could indicate that they are looking for other resting and sleeping places than perches. Why? Red mites like to hide under perches. As the risk of a red mite infection increases, the chickens start to stay away from the perches. In that case the number of floor eggs will probably also be increased (mites in nests).

Host

Every parasite needs a host to survive. The red mite prefers various species of wild birds and the chicken. You will find it regularly in birds' nests. The red mite can also occasionally attack mammals (such as rodents, dogs and cats) and even humans. In optimum conditions an egg will develop into a fully grown red mite in seven days. The red mite sucks blood even in the nymph stage.

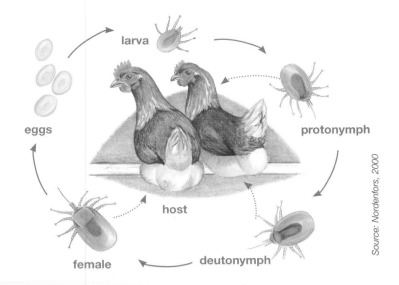

Source: Nordenfors, 2000

Do the red mite test yourself

Red mites can be tracked down by knocking on the system or by scraping in cracks with a knife while holding a white sheet of paper underneath. You can also hang up mite traps in which the mites will hide. Inspect places where red mites are likely to hide daily. In cages these are mainly under the egg protection panel, fastening clips and gutter. In non-caged systems you will find them under perches, under slats, in dry droppings and in laying nests.

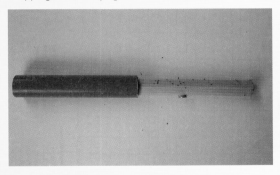

Mite trap. Create a hiding place for red mites. Insert a rod in a dark tube and hang it underneath the perch. After 24 hours, remove the rod and check for red mites.

LOOK-THINK-ACT

Also carry out some covert surveillance during the dark period.

This photo was taken at night with an infrared camera. The chickens should be sleeping peacefully. But as you can see, the hen on the left is picking at itself to stop the itching. This is disturbing other chickens as well.

Index